8/94

PRINTING

WATER-BASED TECHNIQUES

RONI HENNING

WATSON-GUPTILL PUBLICATIONS
NEW YORK

Cover image:
Hugh Kepets, *Columbus I*,
48 x 36¹/₂" (122 x 92.7 cm).
Printed by the author and Greg Radich.
Copyright © 1991, by Hugh Kepets.

Half-title image:
Gretchen Dow Simpson, *Flag 1991*,
37¹/₂ x 30" (95.2 x 76.2 cm).
Published by Pamplemousse Press, New York.

Title-page image:
Ben Benson, *Untitled*,
34 x 46¹/₄" (66.7 x 117.5 cm).
Printed at Noblet Serigraphic, Inc., New York.

Page 6:
Urania Michos, *Untitled*,
20¹/₂ x 26³/₄" (52 x 68 cm).
Printed with oil-based inks by the artist.

Page 8:
Mark Williams, *World Variation*,
34⁵/₈ x 44" (88 x 111.7 cm).
Printed by the author at the Screenprint Workshop.
Copyright © 1987, by Mark Williams.

Page 41:
Ginny, Copyright © The Estate of Alice Neel.
Published by Avocet

Page 50:
Columbus II, Copyright © 1991,
by Hugh Kepets.

Page 53:
Mick Jagger, Copyright © 1994,
the Andy Warhol Foundation
for the Visual Arts, Inc.

Senior Editor: Candace Raney
Associate Editor: Dale Ramsey
Designer: Bob Fillie
Production Manager: Hector Campbell

Copyright © 1994, by Roni Henning

First published in 1994 in the United States by Watson-Guptill
Publications, a division of BPI Communications, Inc. 1515 Broadway,
New York, New York 10036

Library of Congress Cataloging-in-Publication Data
Henning, Roni, 1939—
      Screenprinting: water-based techniques / Roni Henning.
            p. cm.
      Includes bibliographical and index.
      ISBN 0-8230-5644-9 : $29.95
      1. Serigraphy—Technique. I. Title. II. Title: Screen printing.
NE2236.H46   1994
764'.8—dc20

Manufactured in Hong Kong

1 2 3 4 5 / 98 97 96 95 94

This book is dedicated to my husband, John Henning,
who died before its publication. His unique and joyful outlook on life
and his lifelong encouragement of all my endeavors enabled me
to write it. I will always love and miss him.

ACKNOWLEDGMENTS

My first words of thanks go to my daughters, Diane and Dawn, whose love and support sustained me in my grief over my husband's death. My son-in-law, Josué Santiago, also helped me tremendously. For her transcribing of my notes, I thank Julia Marks.

All the prints were beautifully photographed by Maurice Sherman, and the instructional close-up photos, making everything look clear and easy, were the work of Christina Lessa. The location photos were taken by Dan Schierhorst. I greatly appreciate their fine efforts and assistance. Thanks also to Barbara Bartlett and Antonella Natale for demonstrating in these pictures.

This book would never have come about if Marie Dormuth had not introduced me to Greg Radich and water-based ink. They have certainly earned my gratitude. I also greatly appreciate the technical advice I obtained from Pete Ebert of E & A Screen Graphics and Dick Kelsey of T.W. Graphics.

I thank the following printmakers for supplying me with beautiful works from their collections: Andrea Callard, of Avocet; Rand Russell, of Grin Graphics; and Jean Noblet, of Noblet Serigraphic.

Robert Kimbril, of Orion Editions, deserves special mention for generously providing me with images and with encouraging my venture into water-based printing.

I gratefully acknowledge the New York Institute of Technology for providing me with the Screenprint Workshop, where I was able to develop professional water-based printing, and I deeply appreciate the advice of Art Brings, the Institute's environmental consultant, and the support of John Murray, the chairman of the Art Department.

I enjoyed working with all the artists herein, and I heartily thank them for their permission to illustrate their prints. A separate nod of thanks goes to Darra Keeton, David Grubb, Hugh Kepets, and Elsie Manville. Also, my friends Janet DeCecelia, Linda Smukler, and Dorothy Varon gave their much-appreciated support.

I am very grateful to Candace Raney, senior editor at Watson-Guptill, for her confidence in this project, and to Dale Ramsey, associate editor, for his expert editing. Thanks to Bob Fillie, who did a wonderful job of designing the book, and to Hector Campbell, for managing its production.

CONTENTS

PREFACE

It was suggested to me long before I switched to water-based ink that my health was in jeopardy by making screenprints. I have been teaching printmaking and making prints at the New York Institute of Technology's Screenprint Workshop as their master printer-in-residence for eighteen years. The Screenprint Workshop is a unique facility that allows artists to make limited editions of their art in collaboration with the master printer. It also permits the students to have an opportunity to watch prints being made professionally by established and prominent artists. In this way it functions as a teaching facility.

Over the years, the print shop went through many periods of change, and it was during one of these, after completing a forty-color edition of 600 prints, that I started to question what I was doing to myself and the environment—and, of course, to my students. Printers are a rigid breed, and once they have developed a system of doing things that works well, they are reluctant to change. I myself had felt this reluctance. I didn't yet realize that if something is poisoning the environment, it can hardly be considered to be working well, even though the product looks good.

Marie Dormuth—a friend, an artist, and a screenprinting teacher at Parsons School of Design and at Cooper Union in New York—had changed their printmaking departments to a water-based system. She recommended T.W. Graphics ink, and she introduced me to Greg Radich, an illustrator and printmaker. Together, we spent two years working out all the technical problems that would arise in making high-quality large editions with these inks.

Publishers and artists that I work with love the results. Artists in particular enjoy being in a print shop with an art-studio atmosphere, and the school has a much healthier environment for the students.

The purpose of this book is twofold: to showcase the creative, high-quality prints that were made with water-based ink, and to assist serious printers and artists in their transition from an oil-based system. This book should dispel the notion that water-based inks are a poor substitute for the traditional inks that have been used for so long. The art-materials industry continues to focus on developing even better versions of the new inks.

The reader should assume that the prints in this book have been printed with water-based ink. There are some exceptions, which appear primarily in Chapter 3, "Creative Stencil-Making," and they are so noted. There I included some prints that were made with oil-based ink because, after all, the stencil method is the same for both oil- and water-based work. Wherever possible, I used a water-based print alongside the oil-based example to show this.

Most of my research has involved the editions made at the Screenprint Workshop, but I have found other artists and printers that have printed with excellent results using different brands of ink. One of these artists is Andrea Callard, the founder of Avocet, an artists' forum and studio that publishes prints. She introduced me to Rand Russell, a master printer at Grin Graphics who has also created some remarkable editions; some of her work is included in this book.

Finally, I also wanted to demonstrate a practical approach to making a print and to show how to analyze the original art using some of the techniques for making color separations. There are endless possibilities for creating prints that can be explored now that the print shop is a safer, more inviting place.

Chapter 1

A Brief History of Screenprinting

Screenprinting is a process of passing inks through stencils that have been adhered to silk or synthetic fabrics stretched over frames. The use of the stretched fabric, or screen, evolved as a solution to problems inherent in the stencil method of printing. The stencil method is one of the oldest and easiest forms of printing. A design is cut out of a piece of paper or other material and paint or ink is brushed or daubed over the cutout area to print the design. The hand was used as a stencil in prehistoric paintings that were found alongside cave paintings of animals in the Magdalenian caves in the French Pyrénées. Powdered pigment was dusted around the hand to form the negative image.

Elsie Manville, *Artist at Work*,
26 x 37" (66 x 94 cm).
The advent of new photo-
sensitive emulsions made it
possible to print complicated
screenprints like this print,
made with thirty-five hand-
drawn stencils on textured
acetate. It was printed by the
author and Greg Radich in
collaboration with the artist.
Published by Orion Editions,
New York.

More complicated stenciling was found in decorations of Egyptian tombs, and the ancient Romans advertised coming events at their games by stenciling letters on wooden signs. The Japanese and Chinese used the stencil method to print geometric and floral patterns on fabrics.

Fine-art stencil printing is called *pochoir*, a French word for "stencil," and this method is still used today to make prints with watercolor or gouache and brushes.

Although the origins of screenprinting are obscure, it was the Japanese who contributed the most significant advances in the evolution of stenciling between A.D. 500 and 1000. A limitation of stenciling was the inability to print floating shapes, such as the center of a circle, for there was no way to attach such shapes to the main stencil. The Japanese artisans anchored floating shapes to the main stencil by attaching fine strands of silk or human hair to them. This suspended them in place. Using this technique, these artisans were able to create far more intricate designs than before. Their solution to the floating shape problem was to attach the stencil to a piece of fabric to provide a sturdier foundation. This method, the precursor of the modern fixed stencil, was adopted for use by the textile printers in Japan. Medieval British artisans painted negative designs of royal crests and other symbols directly on the fabric with tar. When the tar hardened, it formed a stencil that would not allow pigment to penetrate the fabric. A stiff brush was used to force pigment through the unpainted areas to create colorful symbols on horse trappings and banners.

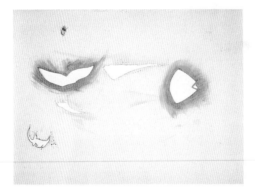
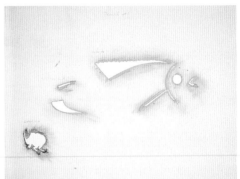

These two stencils, made of wax paper, were used to print part of my pochoir, *Rhinoceros Beetle*. The residue of watercolor remains on the edge of the cutout shapes where the color was printed.

Roni Henning,
Rhinoceros Beetle,
22 x 30" (56 x 76.2 cm).
My pochoir was printed with watercolors and twelve stencils on Arches cold-pressed watercolor paper.

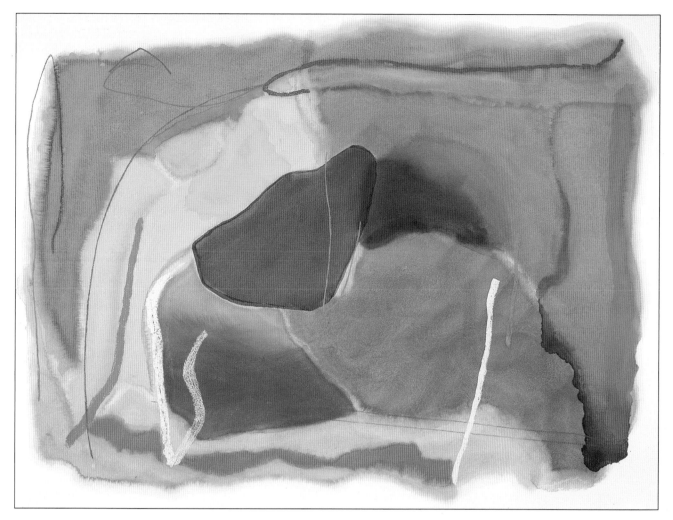

From this point on, the use of fabric to fix a stencil was elaborated on and experimented with, and eventually printers hit on the idea of attaching the fabric to a wooden frame, providing a more precise and controllable tool for the printer. This idea has survived to the present day, since all fabric matrices used in screenprinting are still stretched on frames.

The development of screenprinting was a evolutionary process shared by numerous unknown artisans in the past. One who is known was Samuel Simson, who applied for, and was granted, a patent in England in 1907 for a process of painting designs directly on silk. It was very much like the method used in the Middle Ages, but his process used a glue-like substance that filled the spaces in the fabric, creating a fixed stencil. The printing inks were forced through the uncoated areas with a stiff brush.

Twentieth-century technical advances played an important role in the development of screenprinting. In the 1920s, the squeegee, a flat, rigid board with a flexible rubber edge, was designed to force the printing ink through the fabric with more efficiency and uniformity than was attainable with stiff brushes.

Eventually, synthetic fabrics allowed printers to escape from the expensive use of silk. They could now choose the mesh best suited to their printing requirements. This allowed screenprinters to print designs of increasing complexity and intricate detail. Also, advances in photography led to the development of light-sensitive films and emulsions which could be applied to the screens and turn projected images into stencils on the mesh. Photo-stencil applications were even more efficient than earlier methods and contributed to the development of new printing techniques. Screenprinting proliferated as a commercial process.

Coinciding with some of these technical innovations was the Great Depression, which started in the United States in 1929. Ironically, this disastrous eco-

Larry Zox, *Dexter's Way #1*, 40 x 60" (101.5 x 152.5 cm). The artist worked in collaboration with the author, who was the printer. Larry Zox mixed the colors and supervised the proofing. There are two color states, this print being the first. *Dexter's Way #2* was the second color state. The printing was done on Arches 300-lb. cold-pressed watercolor paper. The publisher was Images Gallery, Toledo, Ohio.

nomic situation provided fertile ground for screenprinting to develop as a fine-art medium in the United States, because of the low overhead costs of operating screenprinting shops. They could be set up and maintained for much less than lithography or intaglio shops. In 1935, printer Anthony Velonis was supported by the government in a Works Progress Administration program to provide jobs for many people, including artists, during the Depression. Velonis brought in prominent artists such as Ben Shahn to emphasize the creative virtues of the screenprint medium. The artists were encouraged to explore the medium, and this helped to build respect for screenprinting.

In 1940, the National Serigraph Society was founded to exhibit and promote screenprinting around the

world, focusing on its accomplishments. Incidentally, it was Carl Zigrosser, then-curator of the Philadelphia Museum of Art, that coined the expression "serigraph," from the Latin word for "silk," *seri*, and the Greek word for "to write," *graphos*. Unfortunately, despite the efforts of Velonis and the National Serigraph Society, screenprinting was still largely considered a commercial process for printing bottle labels and colorful detergent boxes. It took two more energetic developmental pushes before screenprinting would be considered a legitimate fine-art printing medium.

The first push was provided during the 1950s by Lutpold Domberger in Stuttgart, Germany. Like Velonis, he

Opposite page: Tomie Arai, *The Laundryman's Daughter*, 29 x 20" (73.6 x 50.8 cm). Printed in six colors on Rives BFK paper, this print employed a photographic stencil, a significant advance in screenprinting technology. Published by Avocet.

offered his print shop to prominent artists associated with the Op Art movement. Respected artists like Josef Albers and Victor Vasarely combined their artistic visions with Domberger's relentless pursuit of perfection as a screenprinter. They created superior, finely executed serigraphs which were sought by art galleries and collectors around the world. These efforts in Germany, combined with the experimentation of Ben Shahn and Jackson Pollock in the United States, helped to keep the screenprint medium in the forefront of printmaking. This sparked the explosion of creativity in the field, which followed in the 1960s.

The Pop Art movement in general, and Andy Warhol in particular, eliminated the identification of screenprinting as only a commercial process once and for all when Warhol walked into a screenprinting shop with a Brillo box and asked them to duplicate it. He wanted to create a limited edition of mass-produced sculptures called multiples. These reproduced Brillo boxes were exhibited in one of the most exciting and memorable gallery exhibits in New York City, which became a landmark in art history. Roy Lichtenstein, Robert Rauschenberg, and Jasper Johns also used screenprinting to express their Pop Art visions. They pushed the medium in unexplored directions, achieving practically every effect desired by an artist. The successes and popularity of screenprinting in the 1960s encouraged interest in the 1970s in researching more light-sensitive photo emulsions as well as ultrafine mesh screens. These developments provided the printer with unparalleled detail.

In the 1980s, the focus changed from perfection of the print process to an examination of the health effects of the highly toxic solvents and materials used in the process, as well as the impact of these materials on the environment.

WHY WATER-BASED INKS?

Because of the toxic nature of solvent-based printing, a number of protective measures needed to be taken which at once made the process safer for the printer, yet did nothing to protect the environment into which the substances would be eventually released. These

measures, unfortunately, made the process more expensive. They also entailed difficulties in using oil-based inks in schools and colleges, because often the protective measures were inadequate, considering the large number of students printing in very confined spaces. To protect the printer from fumes created by the use of solvents, inks, and emulsion removers, protective gear was used, which varied depending on the product; these included rubber gloves, goggles, barrier creams, and respirators.

Respirators proved to be cumbersome, uncomfortable, and difficult to wear for long periods. A better solution was to install a powerful centralized ventilation system that kept circulating the air in the shop. These measures were very expensive, and only high-volume shops could afford systems that would do a sufficient job. Often, neither respirators nor ventilation systems solved the problem entirely, and everyone in the shop continued to be exposed to toxic fumes. These fumes would cause them to suffer from headaches, nausea, dizziness, and irritation of their respiratory systems, eyes, and skin. Over the course of many years of consistent exposure, serious health problems could arise, affecting the kidneys, liver, and neurological system.

Environmental Factors
These hazards to the individual are compounded as the environment becomes the recipient of toxic waste created by the oil-based shop. A ventilation system may extract hazardous fumes from the shop only to expel them into the outside air for passersby to breathe. Paper towels and rags used to clean up after printing are filled with solvents and inks which can contaminate ground water under landfills. Emulsion residue washed down sinks during screen reclaiming procedures is highly toxic and can also contaminate ground water. There are reclamation systems that hold contaminated water in tanks which evaporate the water, leaving a contaminated sludge that must be hauled away and neutralized. The system itself, as well as the disposal of the contaminated sludge, is a very expensive solution to this problem.

Artists and printers have demanded more information about the products they use as a result of heightened awareness of the health risks involved with the medium. This awareness was due in part to the environmental movement, from the 1970s to the present. A re-evaluation of oil-based technology has ensued from the passage of "Right to Know" laws, coupled with efforts by the Occupational Safety and Health Agency (specifically, OSHA Hazard Communication Standard 29CRF1910-1200), which spearheads the government's enforcement of pollution laws. One result has been that Material Safety Data Sheets, consisting of a manufacturer's report regarding all information about the toxic hazards of its products and how to protect oneself during use, are available upon request by the user. These data also include handling and storage information.

It became clear, as more detailed information became available to consumers, that the only solution to the solvent-based problem was to search for an alternative. Health concerns prompted a revolutionary upheaval in the industry as professionals and educators sought a more nontoxic approach to screenprinting.

The solution was found in existing water-based ink technology that had been used in the textile industry for years. These inks needed to be modified for use on paper, but they had an inherent advantage over oil-based inks in that no solvent was needed for printing or cleanup. As a result of continuing research, the inks are now virtually nontoxic and are considered safe for users and the environment. Of course, all the manufacturer's instructions on handling the inks should always be followed to ensure complete safety.

Though still in their infancy as a fine-art medium, water-based inks have already been used to create professional-quality prints that are indistinguishable from oil-based prints. They are also ideal for classroom use because of their nontoxic nature and ease of use. Complementing the safety of the inks is the research into safer emulsions and reclaimers that are more organically based. Ultimately, people, the industry, and the environment can only benefit from this new technology.

Opposite page:
Elizabeth Osborne,
Winter Still Life,
30 x 22" (76.2 x 56 cm).
This twenty-color pochoir was printed by the author. The stencils were made of wax paper and printed with watercolor. Published by Orion Editions.

Chapter 2

Making the Screen

Just as in any technical discipline (screenprinting being both creative and technical), equipment and supplies affect the quality of the result. Screenprinters and manufacturers are always trying to improve on their products and materials for making and stretching screens. A screen consists of fabric that is stretched tightly over a frame and adhered with glue, staples, or nails. Frames are available in wood or metal, although wood still remains the material of choice by most printers, because of its lower cost and versatility. Since the frame is the support, it must be strong enough to withstand the tension of the stretched fabric, without warping.

Tom Martin, *Swimmer*, 24 x 30" (61 x 76.2 cm). A coarser mesh of 196 monofilament white polyester was used to print this work. This is because the colors had to be printed with a heavier amount of flat opaque ink. It was printed by the author at the New York Institute of Technology's Screenprint Workshop, using T.W. Graphics water-based ink (1000 line).

The frame of the screen should be built (from the inside dimension) four inches larger on all four sides than the image.

METAL FRAMES

Metal frames are usually used by commercial print shops for precision printing of electronic parts, printed circuits, and so on.

Metal frames are available in steel or aluminum and are not made by hand. They are very stable and do not warp. This makes them ideal when a screen must be stretched with the highest possible tension. This tight stretch aids in the application of the stencils, and it prevents distortions. Because the mesh is a fabric, it has some "give" as the squeegee moves over it. A less tensely stretched screen will give substantially. This not only causes a change in the stencil, it also affects the way the ink prints. As the squeegee pushes ink through the mesh of the stencil, the screen should be so tight that it will release from the paper. This allows a nice even application of ink. A loose screen remains in contact with the printed paper and causes unwanted inconsistencies in the ink, like water or rainbow shapes.

Steel frames are very durable, but can be difficult to handle in large sizes because of their weight. Aluminum frames are lightweight and have welded corners for strength. All metal screens should be stretched on a machine and the fabric glued. The top of the frame is sandblasted or roughened by grinding to achieve good fabric adhesion.

There are metal frames from which the fabric is easily removable, so one frame can be used with many different fabrics. The mesh is placed over the metal frame, which has grooves and bolts for holding and stretching. Four locking bars are placed over the fabric on all four sides and snapped into the grooves, holding the mesh in place. The bolts are tightened, causing the mesh to stretch. The advantage of this method is that the screen can be stretched very tightly, and yet the frame is instantly reusable. Just snap the fabric out when you finish printing and snap another piece in.

WOOD FRAMES

Wood frames can be easily made and used to print any range of things, from tee shirts to fine-art editions.

Pine and cedar are two good choices for wood frames. They are light, and cedar is also water-resistant. Since the screen will be washed many times in applying and removing stencils, this is an excellent advantage. Wood frames can be hand-stretched or machine-stretched like metal frames.

Machine stretching of wood or metal usually requires holding the fabric over the frame with clamps and the use of an air compressor. These clamps are placed side-by-side on all four sides of the screen—perhaps as many as five clamps on each side, depending on the size of the frame. The fabric is attached to each clamp and tightened. The clamps move back and forth on individual bars. When the compressor is turned on, the clamps move away from the frame, pulling the fabric and stretching it tightly. The frame adhesive is applied at this time and allowed to dry before the clamps are removed.

Building a Wooden Frame

You should build a frame according to the size of the image. There should be at least four inches from the inside of the wood frame to the beginning of the image that you want to print. Therefore, if your printing area is 16 x 20", the inside of the frame should be 24 x 28". The thickness of the wood depends on the size of the screen. A small 24 x 28" screen requires 2 x 3" strips of wood, while a larger screen, say 60 x 80", would need 2 x 4" strips. There are several ways to join the wood at the corners:

1. Butt joint
2. Mitered joint
3. Lap joint
4. Tongue-and-groove joint

Butt Joint. This joint is the easiest to construct. The wood can even be cut to size at the lumberyard. Using epoxy and nails or screws, simply place the sides together to make a corner. Put the epoxy on the end of one of the pieces of wood and use nails that are long enough to penetrate the first piece of wood and halfway into the second. Use two or three nails per corner and make sure you maintain a right angle. With

There are four different joints connecting the wood frame that can be used:

1. The butt joint simply places two pieces of wood next to each other at right angles to make a corner.

2. The mitered joint has the end of the wood sawed off at a 45° angle.

3. The lap joint interlocks by sawing halfway into the wood and creating two lips.

4. The tongue-and-groove joint has negative and positive ends that fit together like a puzzle. This is a very sturdy connection. ·

This extreme closeup of the weave of monofilament (top) and multifilament (bottom) polyester fabrics shows the difference between them. The monofilament is woven with single-strand threads. Each of the multifilament's threads is made up of many strands twisted together to make one.

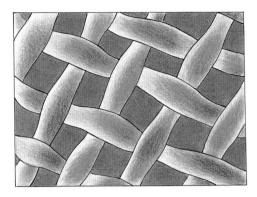

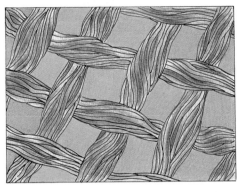

screws, you must drill part of the way into the wood and then finish with screws and a screwdriver.

Mitered Joint. The mitered joint is made by sawing the ends of the wood in a perfect 45° angle. These can also be precut at the lumberyard. Care should be taken to use a miter box to cut the angles correctly so that they will fit flush with each other. The ends are then glued and secured with corrugated nails. The object is to make a frame that is strong and sturdy enough to withstand the tension of the stretched mesh. The frame should have strong 90° angles and not warp or wobble.

Lap Joint and Tongue-and-Groove Joint. Both of these joints are cut so that they fit into each other, making them very stable; the tongue-and-groove is the most stable of them all.

CHOOSING THE RIGHT FABRIC

There are a variety of fabrics used to stretch screens. In the past, silk was so commonly used it lent its name to the term "silkscreening." Today the printing method is referred to as "screenprinting," for silk is rarely used. One reason is that it loses its tautness with frequent use; another is that the bleach used in reclaiming the photo stencil destroys it.

Nylon is good for stretching screens, but the best fabric is monofilament or multifilament polyester. It is very strong and stable when stretched. Most fine-art editions are printed with monofilament. Multifilament is used more in the textile industry.

Monofilament fabric is made up of single strands of polyester, and multifilament fabric consists of threads that are actually many strands wound together. Monofilament is easier to clean and is my first choice for printing with water-based ink. These fabrics are available at screen-supply companies and even some art-supply stores.

The size of the fabric mesh is calculated by the number of threads per inch. The more numerous the threads, the finer the mesh; the fewer the threads, the coarser the mesh. The space between the threads is the mesh opening. The image that is to be printed should determine the fineness or coarseness of the mesh you select.

A finer mesh is used to print detail and halftones that require thin deposits of ink. A coarser mesh is used to print flatter, open shapes with a heavier deposit of ink. A coarse mesh in monofilament polyester would be listed as 160–180 threads per inch and a finer mesh would range between 200–260. There are meshes of over 300 used to print very fine halftones. The best range for water-based ink is 200–260, but I have seen very fine four-color process printing on 300 mesh.

The monofilament is white, yellow, or orange. The yellow and orange fabric was designed for use with direct photo stencils. The color prevents light from bouncing when the stencil is exposed to an ultraviolet light. If the light bounces or scatters, the exposure will not be even. White fabric is used mostly for stencils directly hand-drawn on the screen.

STRETCHING THE SCREEN

Most printers have their favorite way to stretch a screen, and most of them are effective. The method that I recently saw at E & A Screen Graphics, in New York, was very efficient and made a very tight screen.

Start with a frame made with a tongue-and-groove joint. Do not nail it; just put it together. Cut the fabric so that

1

1. All the supplies are gathered together before stretching the screen: four pieces of pine cut on the ends with a tongue-and-groove joint; one piece of orange polyester monofilament cut four inches larger than the frame on all four sides; a staple gun and staples; and two kinds of tape: fabric and wide plastic.

2. After the screen has been stapled on one side, the fabric and tape are pulled tightly into the next corner, and the second side is stapled at right angles to the first.

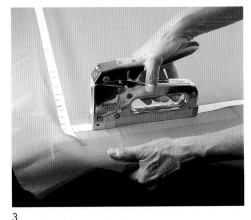

3

4

3. Using a block of wood held in one hand with the fabric over it, pull the fabric and block very tightly away from the frame. While holding it, lay the fabric tape along the frame on top of the fabric and staple the third side.

4. After all four sides are stretched and stapled, the excess fabric is cut off with a mat knife.

5. The finished screen should be tight, having no "give" when you touch it. The next step is to put tape over the staples, using wide plastic tape (similar to duct tape, which also can be used).

5

Above: Andrea Callard,
Old Wood/New Life,
30 x 22" (76.2 x 56 cm).
This work was printed by the artist
in eight colors with screens made of
white 230 (threads per inch) polyester
monofilament. Published by Avocet.

Opposite page:
Whitfield Lovell, *The Dress*,
30 x 22" (76.2 x 56 cm).
Screens of white 230 monofilament
were used. The printing was a
collaboration between the artist and
Andrea Callard. The artist drew the
color separations on frosted acetate
with crayons, and it was printed on
Rives BFK paper. Published by Avocet.

it is four inches larger than the frame on
all four sides. Lay it over the frame. Cut
a piece of fabric tape and lay it over the
mesh on one side. Staple the tape and
mesh on one corner. Pull the fabric
along the wood tightly to the next
corner and, with the tape lying over it,
staple the next corner. Now fill in all the
staples along that side. Repeat this on
an adjoining side. Make sure you pull
the fabric tightly to the next corner or
it will not work. Staple this side. You
should now have two adjoining sides
stapled.

Now use a block of wood to give you
leverage and stretch the fabric across
the frame from one side, preferably the
wider side. Hold the block of wood
with one hand with the fabric held
lightly over it, and pull as tightly as you
can. With the other hand lay the tape
over the part of the frame that the fabric
is being pulled over. Now staple this
side. As you staple, move the block
of wood along the side to maintain
tightness. Repeat this procedure on the
last side.

The fabric tape is used to prevent the
fabric from tearing as you staple. After
all four sides are stapled, cut the excess
fabric off with a mat knife or razor
blade. Nail all four tongue-and-groove
corners. Tape over the staples and fabric
with wide white plastic tape. Be sure
also to tape the inside of the screen
halfway up the wood and halfway onto
the mesh to prevent ink from getting
into the groove where the wood and
mesh are joined. If the screen is
stretched correctly, there should not be
any hills and valleys as you run your
hand over the screen. Many printers
like to shellac or varnish the wood to
protect it. I have never found this necessary; I rely on the plastic tape.

Once the screen is stretched and
taped, the fabric is roughed up and
degreased with an abrasive powdered
cleanser such as Ajax or Comet. Screen
supply shops sell special degreasers,
but they are usually more toxic than
these household cleansers. Degreasing
the screen makes the photo emulsions
adhere to the mesh better.

Chapter 3

Creative Stencil-Making

In the past, screenprinting was thought of only as a way to print flat shapes of opaque color, unlike etching or lithography, which can produce any range of printed textures and tones. A screenprint could deposit a thick layer of brilliant color on many different surfaces such as glass, foil, fabric, cardboard, and paper. The look of the print could be matte or gloss depending on the choice of ink. Today, with new technology and materials, no complex image or textural effect is beyond the range of a screenprint. With screenprinting's richness of color, it is now one of the most versatile printing methods. Achieving complexity starts with a clear understanding of stencil methods and some thoughtful planning.

Harrison Burns,
Raritan River,
22 x 30 " (56 x 76.2 cm).

PLANNING THE PRINT

You begin by deciding to pursue one of three approaches to developing the print, each being creatively different.

Original Art

Stencils can be made directly from an original painting, drawing, or photograph. There is no flexibility or experimentation involved. The object is to create a print that is as true to the original art as the medium will allow.

Ideas into Prints

You can develop an idea into a drawing as a plan for your stencil. Make several preliminary sketches before deciding on the final piece. The size and colors should be resolved before the stencils are made. An accurate drawing makes it easier to determine the number of stencils necessary to make the print.

A screenprint is made by printing one color at a time on all the sheets of paper. Each color must have its own stencil. Since a stencil represents a color separation, your drawing is a means of breaking down the art into different colors, tones, or values so that they may be applied to the screen and printed. If you plan a print having three colors—say, yellow, red, and green—a separate stencil must be planned for each color (that is, a stencil for yellow, one for red, and one for green).

Being Open to Chance

The third approach is less rigid, for it involves letting the image emerge from the printing of the stencils. First, you should familiarize yourself with the different types of stencils. Decide on one or two and invent the image as you make each stencil and print each color. Experiment with the color.

By this approach the artist freely develops an image from the process of printing. It can be risky, but it is also very creative.

DIRECT STENCILS

One of the easiest methods of making a stencil is to paint directly onto a screen with a screen filler or blockout material. This turns the screen itself into a stencil. The screen filler that I recommend is a liquid photo emulsion that can be obtained at any screenprinting supply house. The consistency can be diluted with water to make painting easier. A variety of materials such as brushes, sponges, or pieces of illustration board are used to apply it.

There is an important difference between this filler and the standard water-soluble blockouts and fillers used with oil-based inks. Water-based inks will dissolve the standard blockouts and fillers, but when the photo emulsion is hardened, it is resistant to water. Daylight will harden the emulsion, but it requires a long period of time. Ultraviolet lamps that are used in the screen preparation (see Chapter 4) will harden the emulsion in four or five minutes.

When you paint the emulsion on the screen, you are working in the negative. The emulsion blocks the screen, and

PLANNING THE PRINT:
The three-color print on the left must be printed with three different stencils for the separate colors—a stencil for red, one for yellow, and one for green.

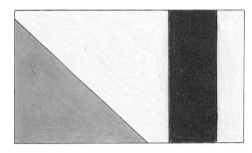

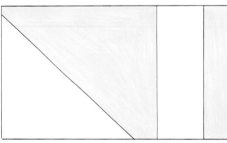

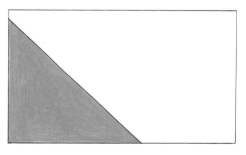

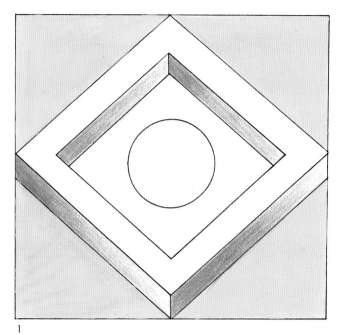

1

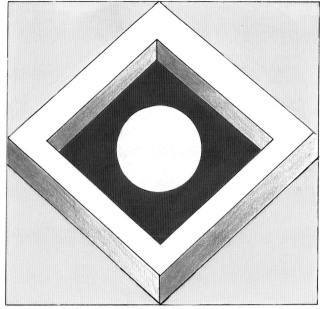

2

the ink prints only in the unpainted, unblocked area. So, for example, if you want to print a circle, draw the circle on the screen with a pencil and then paint everything *except* the circle with screen filler.

Work on the back or the flat side of the screen, which will be in contact with the surface you are printing on. This keeps the inside of the screen smooth and free of any lumps that painting the filler may cause. Such lumps, of course, would interfere with the pull of the squeegee when printing.

The fineness of the mesh of the screen is also important. (The different types of mesh were discussed in Chapter 2 on building and stretching a screen.) When the mesh is a fine weave, the filler builds up more thickly. A thick filler is strong when it is hardened, but it is more difficult to avoid lumpy results. Painting on two thinner coats is preferable. But take note that *very* thin coats will break down when printing, allowing dots of ink to pass onto the paper in unwanted areas. Not hardening the screen sufficiently will cause the same thing to happen.

Creating Straight Edges with Screen Filler

When the print requires a sharp, clean edge, use a ruler, tape, and small pieces of cut illustration board. Painting the edge freehand is too difficult.

1. STRETCHED SCREEN
2. PHOTO EMULSION (SCREEN FILLER)
3. TRANSPARENT TAPE
4. ILLUSTRATION BOARD

To make a square, for example, draw the square on the back of the screen using a pencil and ruler. Place a piece of transparent tape on the inside of the lines on two opposite sides. Press the tape down firmly; any bubbling will allow the filler to seep under and cause a ragged edge. A small amount of emulsion is pulled along the length of the tape on the outside edge with a sharp piece of illustration board. The board should be one or two inches square. Good, firm pressure is used, and the illustration board is kept slanted to help push the filler into the screen. Be careful to cover the tape only halfway so that the filler does not go inside the square, where the mesh is to remain open. (If this happens, it can be easily removed with water.)

After two sides of the square are thus coated and dried, the tape can be removed. The edge will be sharp and smooth. The same process is repeated on the two remaining sides. After the tape has been removed from the last two sides, lay in the screen filler wherever the mesh is still open surrounding the square. In other words, the screen should be blocked everywhere except

DIRECT STENCILS:

1. A screen with a circle drawn on it.

2. The area surrounding the circle is painted with screen filler. Now the ink will print only through the circle.

CREATING STRAIGHT EDGES OF A SQUARE:

1. Draw the square on the screen with a pencil and place transparent tape on the inside of the lines on two opposite sides.

2. The emulsion screen filler is pulled across the tape with a sharp piece of illustration board.

3. After the screen filler is dry, the tape is carefully removed to reveal a sharp, clean square.

1

2

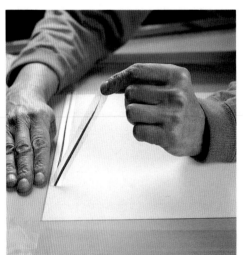

3

Opposite page:
Jerry Schur, *Bora Bora*, 37³/₄ x 30" (95.9 x 76.2 cm). Printed by the author at the Screenprint Workshop with oil-based ink, this is a good example of a reduction print. The stencil method works with either oil or water-based ink. The paper is two-ply Lenox 100.

the square. Use many pieces of board, for the edge loses its sharpness with use. Making two sides of the square at a time ensures that the corners will be perfect.

The best use for this stencil method is *reduction printing*. The prints of Jerry Schur are an excellent example of this method (see pp. 31-33).

Reduction Printing with Screen Filler
The beauty of reduction printing is the use of only one screen. A reduction print relies on the blocking or reducing of the open mesh of the screen every time a color is printed. This procedure follows the order in which the colors are to be printed, which must be predetermined.

Start with a clean open screen and make a line drawing of the image on paper. This drawing is used as a reference as the print progresses. The size of the print is drawn on the back of the screen. Block it out with the screen filler exactly the way the square was made.

Usually the colors are printed with the lightest first and the darkest last, because the lighter colors are more transparent and do not retain their intensity when you try to print them over a darker, more opaque color. After each color is printed, some part of the open mesh of the stencil through which the ink passed is blocked out on the screen with filler. You are reducing the amount of open mesh every time a color is printed. Thus, with this method, the last and darkest color is printed by the smallest amount of open area on the screen.

Each color is printed in exact register on top of the color that preceded it, and the surface of the print gets thicker with the buildup of the colors. The print actually takes on a slight relief quality as it progresses. Many times, the screen is never moved from its position on the printing table. This makes it easy to register each color with the preceding one. Simply look through the open mesh of the screen to see if it is printing in the right place. A small section of the print *Mt. Lyle* is used to demonstrate how the screen was blocked out with filler after each color was printed (p. 33).

Jerry Schur, *Mt. Lyle*, 28½ x 36" (72.4 x 14.2 cm). This forty-two color reduction print was made with screen filler and printed in soft gray tones of very close value on two-ply Lenox 100 paper.

An accurate line drawing of *Mt. Lyle* acts as a map for blocking out each color. I have isolated a small section of this drawing with an orange square to simplify how this print was made (see opposite).

REDUCTION PRINTING:

This series of five drawn screens represents the different colors planned in the orange square. The colored area is the amount that the screen has been blocked out with screen filler.

Screen #1 is a blocked-out square that the first color will print through. This is the lightest color.

Screen #2 is made by blocking out the area where color #1 is to remain unaltered. This is done by using the line drawing as a guide to where color #1 should remain. At the same time, the open area that's left will be used to print color #2.

In screens #3, #4, and #5, this process is repeated. Each preceding color is blocked out according to the line drawing on the screen to create the shape of the next color. The open area of the screen is reduced as each color is printed and blocked out.

Screen #5 represents the last color and the smallest amount of open area on the screen.

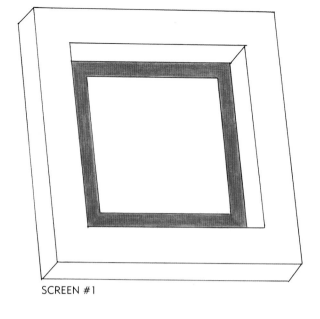

SCREEN #1

SCREEN #2

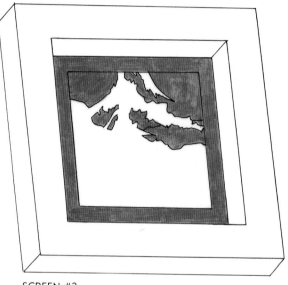

SCREEN #3

SCREEN #4

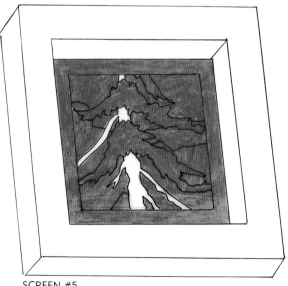

SCREEN #5

INDIRECT STENCILS

Indirect stencils are made of separate materials known as plates, positives, or films. They are a means of separating the various colors in the image into forms that can be applied to the screen and printed. Unlike the direct stencil method, there are several different types of indirect stencils. Each type is chosen for its ability to reflect and translate the style of the image that is to be printed.

The term "hard-edged" refers to art that has no soft or textural edges. For instance, the prints of Red Grooms and Philomena Marano are all hard-edged. They were made with knife-cut stencils.

Style of Image	Stencil Recommendation
HARD-EDGED (SHARP)	KNIFE-CUT STENCIL
SOFT, TEXTURAL	HAND-DRAWN STENCIL
PHOTOGRAPHIC	PHOTO-POSITIVE STENCIL

Knife-Cut Stencils

Knife-cut stencil film is a thin sheet of soft, transparent material laminated to a clear-plastic backing. The soft film layer is cut with a stencil knife and peeled away, leaving the plastic backing intact. The stencil knife can be a fixed blade for cutting straight lines, or a swivel type for cutting curves and circles. Care should be taken to cut only the top layer and not the backing, and a good sharp knife used with light pressure will ensure this.

There are two films commonly in use: Amberlith, which is orange, and Rubylith, which is red. The Amberlith is a little easier to see through, but both work very well. When the film is cut and peeled, the edge remains sharp and clean, making it a good choice for hard-edged imagery. These films are the best choice to use with water-based inks and are available at all print supply houses and most art supply stores.

All the indirect stencil methods discussed in this chapter, including knife-cut stencil film, involve a two-step process. After the stencil is cut, it is applied to the screen, which has been prepared with a photo emulsion. (The complete process of coating emulsion onto the screen and shooting the stencil is covered under screen preparation in Chapter 4.)

A stencil for each color in the original art is cut out of a separate piece of film. Because it is a positive film, everything that prints remains as film, and everything that does not is cut and peeled away. For example: If a blue circle is to be printed, place your Rubylith film over your drawing of the circle. Cut and peel the film everywhere outside the blue circle. The remaining film should exactly correspond to the blue form you want to print.

Just as with the direct stencils, the color order is very important. You should progress from light to dark. Equally important is the registration of the color separations. In order to ensure

that each color is printed in the correct place on the paper, there must be some form of registration.

Registration of Stencils. One method of registration, which serves to guide placement of the colors during the printing process, is with registration crosses. These crosses can be bought in any art store in the form of tape that is placed on the borders of the original art. Each stencil is placed over the original art, and the crosses are added to the stencil to match the crosses underneath. This procedure is followed with all the stencils. The finished stencils, one for each color, are placed on a light table (see p. 51) one over the other. They should fit together like a jigsaw puzzle. Light from the table should not leak through the layers of the separate stencils. When this happens, the light shows along misaligning edges. If you are working with Rubylith film, you can simply correct this by recutting the piece that does not fit.

A master drawing is another method of registration. The artist makes a

Above: Philomena Marano, *Clock and Chutes*, 29 x 41" (73.6 x 104 cm). In another example of a print made with knife-cut stencils, Ms. Marano deals with one of her favorite themes, amusement parks—and Coney Island in particular. Oil-based ink was used.

Opposite page: Red Grooms, *1776*, 26¹/₂ x 34³/₄" (67.3 x 88.2 cm). This print has ten oil-based colors that were printed with Rubylith stencils. The original was cut-and-pasted construction paper.

1. Cutting a straight edge with Rubylith film using a stencil knife and a ruler. The matte or dull side of the film should be on top.

2. Peeling away the Rubylith film of the area that does not print. The film that is left represents the color that will print. In this case, it is the brown border of a Jack Youngerman print.

1

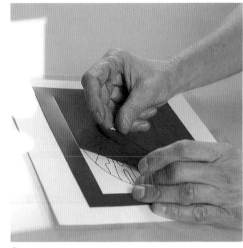

2

Roni Henning, *Eskimo Lizard*, 26¼ x 34" (66.7 x 86.3 cm). Printed by the artist on Arches Cover paper.

detailed drawing as a first stencil. This becomes an accurate guide for all succeeding stencils to align with. Often this is the preferred method with soft, hand-drawn stencils. The master drawing may even be printed first and the color separations drawn directly from it.

Trapping. Stencils must be cut to compensate for the expansion and contraction of the paper due to changes in humidity and the stretch of the mesh when printing. To prevent this, each color separation must be overcut 1/32 of an inch larger where it comes in contact with the following color. This is called *trapping*, and it is another reason that the color order of printing is important. Making a color "trap" under another will ensure that the white of the paper will not show between the colors.

RUBYLITH FILM
STENCIL KNIFE
REGISTRATION CROSSES

The following procedure was used in making the Jack Youngerman print (pp. 38-39) with knife-cut stencils.

The original art is a small maquette that the artist made by gluing cut pieces of color-aid and construction paper together. The print was to be much larger than the original, so a scaled-up line drawing of the desired size was made. The demonstration steps here are a smaller version of the final print.

Since the original has only four colors, the color order is easy.

1. Blue ellipse
2. Brown border
3. Sienna
4. Black

Each color is cut from a separate piece of Rubylith film. Because the blue is first, it is overcut to trap under the sienna and the black. The second stencil —the brown border—is cut exactly on the outside edge and trapped on the inside edge under the sienna brown. The third stencil—the sienna brown—is cut exactly on the border of the outside brown, exactly next to the blue and underneath the black. The final, black stencil is cut exactly to size all around and printed on top of the blue.

Two different types of knives for cutting stencils: a swivel knife (top) for cutting circles and an X-acto knife (bottom) for straight lines. A skilled practitioner can even use a razor blade.

On the left is a blue circle. On the right is a Rubylith stencil that corresponds to the blue circle and is an exact copy.

Registration crosses look like targets and come in the form of tape. All good art stores carry them.

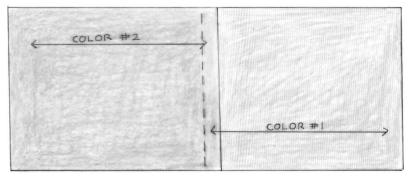

TRAPPING:

Color #1 is made slightly larger so the second color will overlap it. This form of trapping one color under the next ensures that the white of the paper cannot show through between the colors. This can happen if the color separations were cut for an exact fit next to each other and it is caused by the expansion and contraction of the paper and screen.

KNIFE-CUT STENCILS:

A small maquette made by Jack Youngerman as a model for his large screenprint.

A line drawing of the maquette.

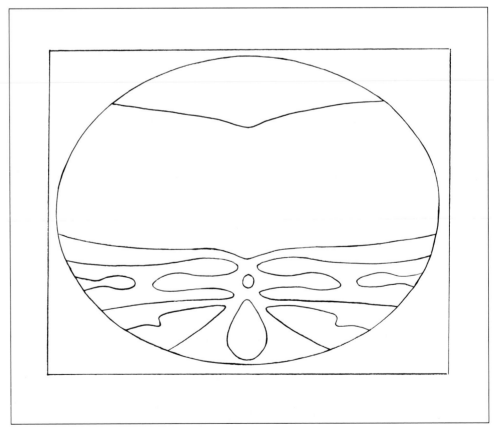

KNIFE-CUT STENCILS:

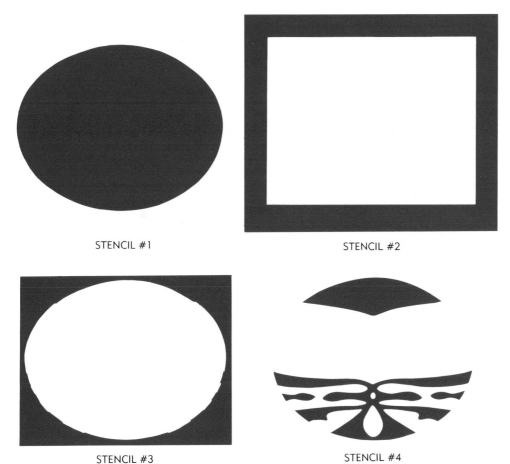

STENCIL #1

STENCIL #2

STENCIL #3

STENCIL #4

These four Rubylith stencils represent the four colors of the Youngerman print.

Stencil #1 is an ellipse. It is overcut slightly so the next stencil will trap on top of it. It represents the color blue.

Stencil #2, the border, is cut exactly on the outside edge and trapped on the inside edge under the next stencil. It represents the color brown.

Stencil #3 is cut exactly, except where it meets the black and traps underneath it. This is the stencil for the color sienna.

Stencil #4 is cut exactly to size. This is the last stencil and represents the color black.

The finished Jack Youngerman print. All the colors match the original maquette and were supervised by the artist during the proofing and printing.

Jack Youngerman, *Untitled*, 45 x 53" (114.3 x 134.6 cm). Printed by the author and Steve Maiorano using oil-based inks.

Hand-Drawn Stencils

Paintings, drawings, pastels, and watercolors usually have some areas of texture, blending, and continuous tone. ("Continuous tone" refers to the smooth gradation of color from light to dark.) Hand-drawn or painted stencils are the best choice for creating prints with these qualities. The prints of Elizabeth Osborne, Alice Neel, and Elsie Manville are good examples of prints with continuous tone and texture.

Hand-drawn and painted stencils are made by drawing directly onto separate sheets of transparent or translucent acetate. Textured or smooth acetate may be used. The rough surface of the textured acetate, or tooth, creates texture as you draw on it. It is the most versatile of the two types. The smoother acetate is primarily used for painting flat, irregular shapes. A variety of means can be used to draw on the acetate to achieve different effects—spray paint, pen and ink, wood rubbings, opaque paint, and so on. In addition, painted areas can be scratched with razor blades or stencil knives to create other textural effects. These stencils must be drawn or painted opaquely in order to transfer them to the screen. Hand-drawn stencils are an indirect positive method. What you paint or draw on the acetate is what will print. For example, a painted black line on a piece of acetate will become the open part of the screen through which any color may be printed. The process of transferring the painted acetate stencils to the screen is described in detail in Chapter 4.

Elizabeth Osborne, *Still Life*, 29 1/2 x 37 1/2" (75 x 95.2 cm). This print features many blended colors that required over thirty hand-drawn color separations to create them. Printed with oil-based inks by the author and Dawn Henning-Santiago.

Alice Neel, *Ginny*,
39¹/₂ x 25" (100.3 x 63.5 cm).
This print of the artist's
daughter-in-law also used
hand-drawn stencils, but it is
much simpler. The texture in
the clothes and hair were
created by painting lithographer's opaquing fluid on
acetate in a diluted form that
beaded up in a different
texture. Transparent oil-based
inks were printed on top of this
texture, and the stencil for the
lines was made with a brush
and opaque paint.

Opposite page: A variety of textures can be made with different materials on acetate: (1) spray paint, (2) pen and ink, (3) rubbings on wood, (4) rubbings on wire mesh, (5) shapes painted with lithographer's opaque, (6) china marker, (7) a sponge and paint, and (8) paint scraped with a razor blade. All these textures must be made opaque in order to be transferred to the screen.

Below:
Andrea Callard, *Barn Theater*, 22 x 30" (56 x 76.2 cm). The stencils were made by rubbing black crayons on tracing paper over wood to get the wood texture. The work was printed in ten colors by the artist in 1985 and published by Avocet.

Continuous Tone with Hand-Drawn Stencils. Continuous tone can be printed in one step by the photo-positive method described later, or as follows by a more involved hand-drawn method. A texture can be drawn on acetate with a black china marker in a continuous tone, from heavier amounts of marker to lighter amounts. Normally, the mesh of the screen that the ink prints through is evenly porous, allowing the ink to pass through it in a solid, flat way. The stencil made with china marker on acetate will control the area that the ink will pass through. When the stencil is transferred to the screen, the black opaque drawing becomes the open mesh area, and the transparent acetate becomes the area that blocks the screen. The ink is now able to print through the open mesh which corresponds to the china marker drawing with its heavier and lighter buildup. This is the first step to creating continuous tone.

It takes four to five drawn stencils to create the transition from light to dark.

The first stencil is the lightest color and has the most detailed texture. The second is drawn with less texture and is printed on top of the first color one shade darker. Each successive stencil has diminishing texture and is printed in progressively darker shades. This then appears to give the illusion of one color that blends from light to dark. This process was used to make the color separations for Elsie Manville's print *Tea and Lemon* (pp. 46-49), because it can reproduce the continuous tone quality of the original oil painting.

MATERIALS

TEXTURED ACETATE
BLACK CHINA MARKER

The painting is analyzed and the number of colors is determined. This print will require thirty-five colors. (The analysis of a painting and the logic of color separations are covered at the end of this chapter.) A master drawing of the entire painting is made by the artist using black china markers on textured

1

2

3

4

5

6

7

8

A black painted line (left) on a sheet of acetate. A screen showing the open part (right) corresponds to the painted line. On acetate, the line is a positive image. When it is transferred to the screen, the positive becomes the open mesh that any color can print through.

CREATING CONTINUOUS TONE WITH HAND-DRAWN STENCILS:

Top: These four hand-drawn stencils were made with black china marker and acetate.

1. This drawing has the most detail. It corresponds to the lightest pink rectangle.

2. This drawing shows less detail and is printed on top of color #1, one shade darker.

3. Even less detailed, this drawing is printed on top of colors #1 and #2, slightly darker.

4. The darkest color with the least detail is printed on top of #1, #2, and #3. The four color swatches relate to the four hand-drawn stencils.

Bottom: Stencil #1 from above prints the light pink. Stencil #2 combines with it to print the slightly darker pink. Stencils #1, #2, and #3 make the third pink even darker. All four stencils create the transition of pink to red, giving the illusion of continuous tone.

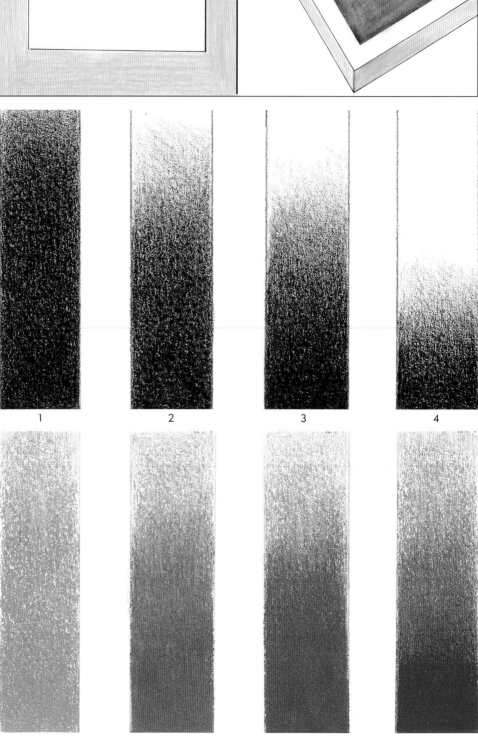

1   2   3   4

acetate. This stencil is drawn with exact detail to be a guide for all the color separations, and it covers the range of all tonalities. A small section of the print is used here to show the number of progressive stencils required to get the total rendering of the teapot. The master drawing is printed first underneath all the other colors in a neutral light gray. The teapot is made up of different colors and shades of those colors rather than of shades of only one color. Stencils are drawn for each of the shades. The most prominent color, the overall turquoise blue, is cut out of a Rubylith film because it is printed as a block of color without texture. Because the tur-

quoise ink is transparent, the textured master drawing will show through it. These first two colors together create the beginning of tonality.

Another Approach. Hugh Kepets' print *Columbus II* (p. 50), is another example of hand-drawn stencil making. In this case, the artist preferred to make all the separations and not just the master. The original art is a buildup of tiny dots of color, very much in the pointillist style of painting. The print is approached in the same way. Working from dark to light, Kepets drew all the stencils, meticulously putting dots on sheets of acetate with magic markers.

Elsie Manville, *Bristol Blue*, 31 1/2 x 37 1/2" (80 x 95 cm). Done exactly as *Tea and Lemon*, with hand-drawn stencils, this image was printed with oil-based inks. In comparing the two prints, you can see that the quality and tonality are equal. Published by Orion Editions, New York.

Elsie Manville, *Tea and Lemon*, 31 x 37" (78.7 x 94 cm). Printed by the author and Greg Radich and published by Orion Editions.

A master drawing of the entire painting *Tea and Lemon*. This drawing is printed in a light gray as a base for the rest of the colors.

This section of the teapot from *Tea and Lemon* shows the tonality and blending of the colors.

Seven stencils were used to create the teapot after the master drawing was printed. The first, a Rubylith stencil, was used to print a transparent turquoise blue and allowed the master drawing to show through.

STENCIL #2 was used to create the shading on the right side of the teapot near the handle.

STENCIL #3, with the most drawing, is printed with a light, chalky blue covering much of the teapot.

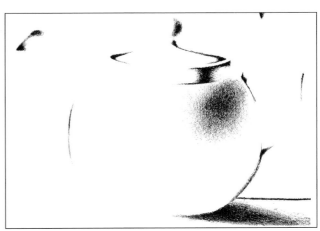

STENCIL #4

STENCIL #5

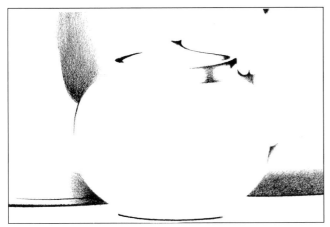

STENCIL #6

STENCIL #7

Slightly darker shades of blue-gray were printed with stencils #4, #5, and #6 on the right of the teapot. Stencil #4 prints on the other objects in the painting as well. The last, stencil #7, corresponds to the light-gray highlight on the left. The white accent was added by the artist by hand with a white pencil.

Hugh Kepets, *Columbus II*, 48 x 36¹/₂" (122 x 92.7 cm). The stencils for the buildup
of tiny dots of color were made by the artist with markers on acetate.

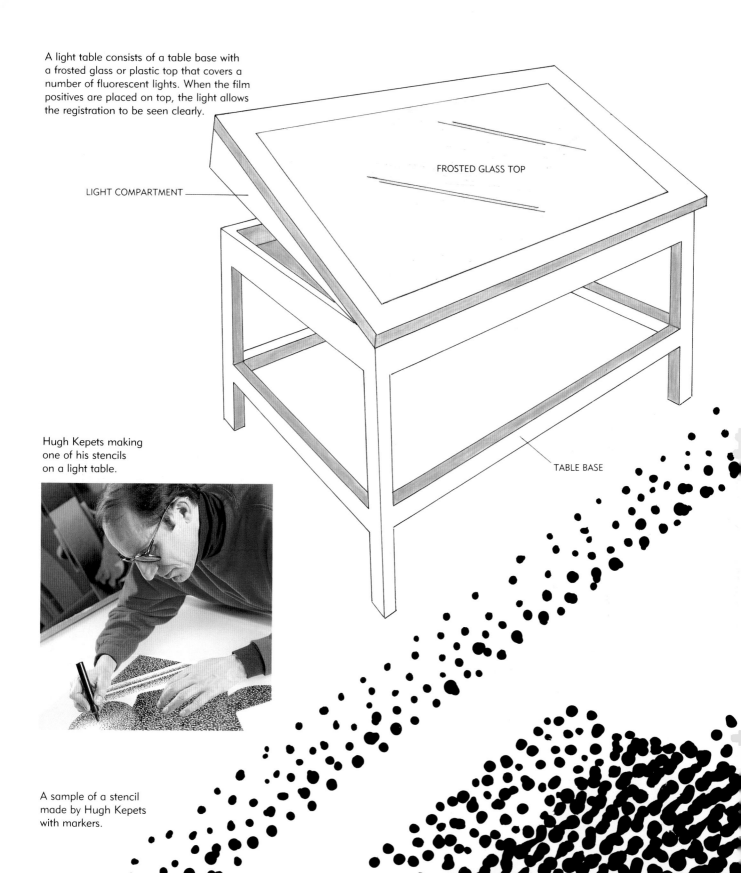

A light table consists of a table base with a frosted glass or plastic top that covers a number of fluorescent lights. When the film positives are placed on top, the light allows the registration to be seen clearly.

FROSTED GLASS TOP

LIGHT COMPARTMENT

TABLE BASE

Hugh Kepets making one of his stencils on a light table.

A sample of a stencil made by Hugh Kepets with markers.

Photo-Positive Stencils

There are two types of photographic image: line and continuous tone. The line image is high-contrast: gray tones disappear, and only black and white remain. Continuous tone, as we have seen, has the full tonal range from dark to light. Since screenprinting is limited in its ability to print tone in one step, it must be simulated. Photo-positive stencils give the illusion of continuous tone.

Photo-positive stencils are made by copying a photo or image with a copy camera onto orthochromatic film. It is important to note that making these stencils requires a working knowledge of a darkroom and a process copy camera. Film positives can also be obtained from photo labs that specialize in this work. Most labs have exhaust systems in operation and now collect waste developer and fixes to reclaim the silver and remove the toxins through evaporation.

The Photographic Process. The copy camera is a large version of an average hand-held camera, with a few additions. There are different makes and models of copy cameras, but the principle in using them is the same. The camera has a copyboard where the photo or image to

be copied is placed and a set of lights that face the copyboard for illumination. The photo or image faces the lens of the camera and the lights; the film, in the back of the camera, is held by vacuum suction. All copy cameras have a glass for viewing the copy and a timer for the exposure.

The orthochromatic film is made of an emulsion-coated transparent plastic. It is a high-contrast film that drops all gray tones and keeps only black on the clear plastic backing when it is shot and developed. This makes it ideal for transferring it to a screen. The black area of the film becomes the open mesh of the screen where ink penetrates. This film can be processed only in a darkroom under a red safelight.

Two types of stencils can be made with ortho film: halftone and posterization. These are discussed below.

The darkroom for developing photo stencils usually consists of a sink for washing the film and trays for the chemicals (developer, stop bath, and fixative). The back of the copy camera usually opens up into the darkroom, which makes it easier to process the film. There should be a place to cut the film, and storage shelves for the supplies.

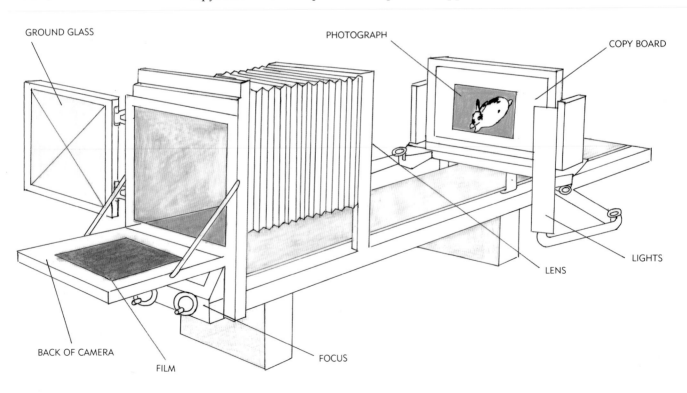

GROUND GLASS

PHOTOGRAPH

COPY BOARD

BACK OF CAMERA

FILM

FOCUS

LENS

LIGHTS

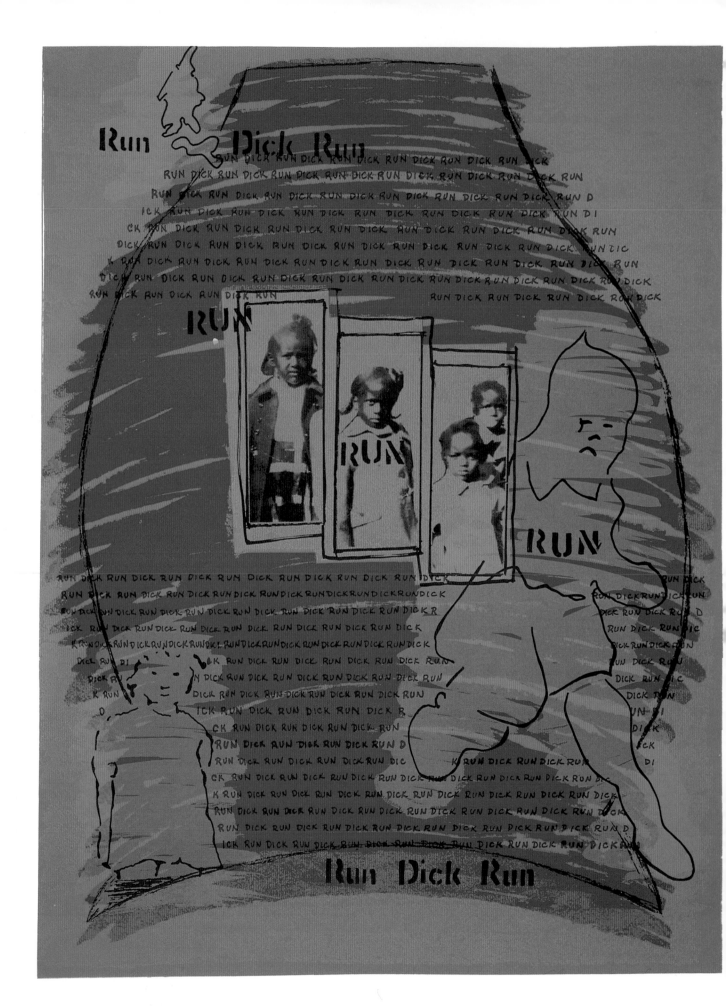

Halftone Stencils. The halftone method makes it possible to copy a photograph without losing continuous tone. This is done by breaking the photo into a regular pattern of dots that corresponds to the light, dark, and gray tones of the photograph. The dots give the illusion of continuous tone. Familiar black-and-white newspaper or magazine photographs provide good examples of how the printed dots create the image. Andy Warhol's *Mick Jagger* and John Murray's *Graf Zeppelin* are screenprinted examples of art created with halftone stencils.

The darkest part of an image reproduced this way contains a 90-percent concentration of dots, while the lightest areas contain only 10 percent. The halftone dot screen comes in different degrees of fineness. A dot screen is made of many dots per square inch. A very fine screen has 100–133 dots per square inch, while a newspaper dot screen is usually 65 dots per square inch. These are referred to as a 65-line screen

and a 100-line screen, respectively.

The reverse of this fine disposition of dots is also possible. The dots can be enlarged so that the image has to be viewed from a distance to be totally understood.

The halftone is achieved by placing the dot screen in contact with the orthochromatic film in the back of the copy camera. The ortho film is placed first with the emulsion side, which has the lightest color of the two sides, facing out. The emulsion side can be determined by folding the back of the film to the front to see the color. This must be done only in the darkroom under a safelight.

The back of the camera is now shut so that the film and dot screen are facing the copyboard holding the image to be copied. In the following illustrations, I have used a photograph of a rabbit on a blanket (pp. 56-61).

Before the film and dot screen are placed in the camera, it is necessary to

Above:
John Murray, *Graf Zeppelin*
24 x 32" (61 x 81.2 cm).
An overall halftone, with dark green printed on top of the other colors. Printed by the artist with oil-based inks.

Opposite page:
Clarissa Sligh, *Run*,
22 x 30" (56 x 76.2 cm).
An edition of thirty was printed with a 65-line halftone screenprinted by the artist and Andrea Callard and was published by Avocet. Water-based Createx ink was used on Rives BFK paper. This makes a good contrast with the oil-based halftone by John Murray, above.

Color photo of a rabbit on a blanket.

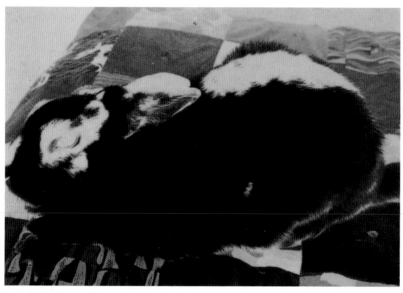

The halftone negative was made with a 65-line dot screen.

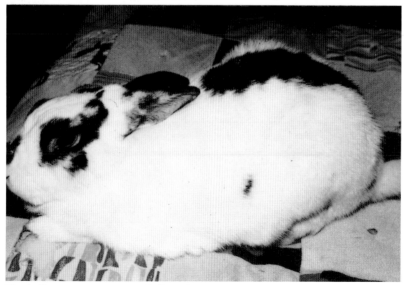

The halftone positive was made from the negative.

determine the size and correct exposure time. Start by looking through the camera's glass viewfinder. Usually you can enlarge the copy up to 300 percent of its original size and reduce it by the same percentage. Shooting the halftone requires test strips to find the best exposure time. Working from ten seconds to one minute, make test strips of various exposure times. Use a small piece of film covered with the dot screen for the first shot. Repeat this with separate pieces of film, each with a larger exposure time. Always shoot the same section of the copy so there is a good comparison between each film. A gray scale can be placed with the copy to help establish how long to develop the film.

The developer for ortho film is sold in two packs, A and B. Each pack is mixed separately with water following the manufacturer's directions. They can be mixed in advance and kept separately. Before shooting your film, the darkroom must be set up, and an equal amount of A is mixed with an equal amount of B to prepare the developer. Next to the tray of developer should be a stop bath, which stops the action of the developer. The third tray contains a fixative. This, as the name implies, fixes the image on the film so that it becomes permanent.

These chemicals are obtained at any screenprinting supply house or graphic arts film supply store. Great care should be taken when you work with chemicals.

Once the test film is shot, remove it from the back of the camera and place it face down in the developer. Turn it over and agitate the tray by moving it slightly with your hand to speed the development. The image should start to appear between 60 and 90 seconds. What you will see is a negative of your image: the darkest areas will correspond to the lightest parts of the picture.

If the developer is cold, the picture will take longer to appear. This is also true when the developer is old. Every time the developer is used, it oxidizes and loses its strength. If the developer is fresh and the image takes longer than three and a half minutes to appear, then your exposure time has not been long enough.

The film should be developed so that it is opaque and not translucent. This is hard to see if you are not familiar with halftone dots. The gray scale will aid you. Make sure the darkest part of the gray scale is the same on the emulsion side of the film as it is on the back. Overdevelopment will produce blotches and cause fingerprints to appear on the film. It will take some practice to familiarize your eye with the correct results.

When the film is ready, remove it from the developer and put it into the stop bath briefly to end the development. Now place it in the fixative. The film will change appearance: the backing will become transparent and the negative image will remain black. Leave the film in the fix for at least two minutes. Remove it and wash it in running water for five minutes. Now dry the film. This can be done on a line with clothespins.

Once the negative is dry, a positive must be made. The negative is placed on the copyboard where the original image was placed. The procedure just outline is repeated, but without the dot screen, because the dots are already in the negative. The positive will require a shorter exposure time, since you are not shooting through the dot screen and the film.

Until the artist or printmaker becomes familiar with the exposure times, test strips should be made. This will save wasting larger pieces of expensive film. Manipulation of the film with the development time and the exposure time is always possible as you gain experience. Allowing for the fact that what you need to transfer to the screen is an opaque image, the darkroom can become a great place to experiment.

There are a number of different screens that can be used to break the photograph into a printable form. Besides halftone, the mezzotint screen is one of them. This works the same way as a halftone screen, but the pattern is random and not uniform, giving the photo stencil a more natural and less mechanical look. Many artists prefer it for this reason. It more resembles the hand-drawn marks of a china marker on textured acetate than the halftone's pattern of dots.

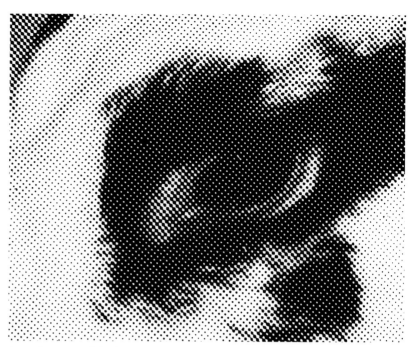

A small section of the halftone positive blown up to a larger dot size.

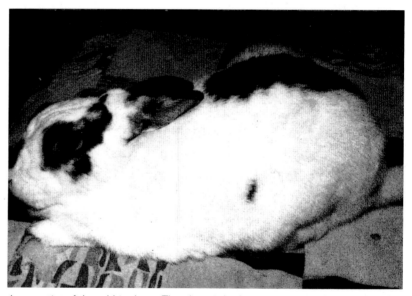

A mezzotint of the rabbit photo. The photo is broken up into a random pattern of dots, giving it a more natural look.

POSTERIZATION:

The rabbit photo is used here to demonstrate posterization.

Step progression #1:
The negative, shot for 20 seconds, copied the lightest area of the photo. A positive was then made from the negative. Color #1, the lightest, a beige, was printed from the positive.

Posterization. Another way to use ortho film to create the illusion of a continuous tone is to *posterize* it. Posterization employs a series, or step-progression, of films that have been shot at different exposure times.

There is no dot pattern. The result of this process is a series of black and clear negatives that look like silhouettes. The longer the exposure, the more silhouetted the image appears. The copy camera can only copy the lightest areas of the image. A twenty-second exposure time will copy whites. Forty seconds will copy the white and light-gray areas. Sixty seconds will copy the white, gray, and dark-gray areas, and so on. In other words, the longer the exposure time, the more the camera is forced to record the middle-gray tones. The dark area of the image cannot be copied because there is no reflected light coming from it onto the film.

Once the negatives are shot, they are developed in A and B ortho developer, the same as the halftone. It is much easier to tell when the film is developed because the dot screen is not there. The

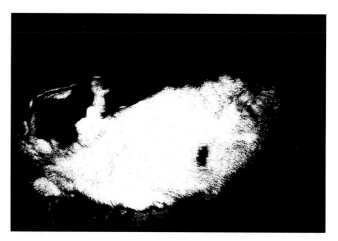

film should be as black on the front or emulsion side as it is on the back. As with the halftone, if the image takes longer than four minutes to appear and the chemicals are fresh, the exposure time is too short. Overdevelopment will produce black blotches and fingerprints.

Proceed to the stop bath and the fixative; use the same method and time as with the halftone. Dry the film, and then return each piece to the copyboard and recopy it to get the positives.

The more exposures of different durations you make, the smoother the transition from light to dark will appear when they are printed. Each of these step progressions represents a different tonality of the original image. When they are printed one on top of the other going from light to dark, the complete image will appear. The print of the rabbit is a good examples of step-progression photo stenciling.

Again, the better you understand film development, the easier it will be to make photo stencils. Still, knowledge gained through trial and error when you use a professional lab is also invaluable.

Step progression #2:
The negative was shot for 40 seconds. Color #2 was printed from the positive, on top of color #1, in a light gray.

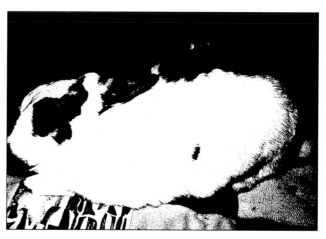

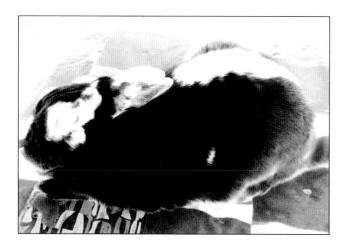 

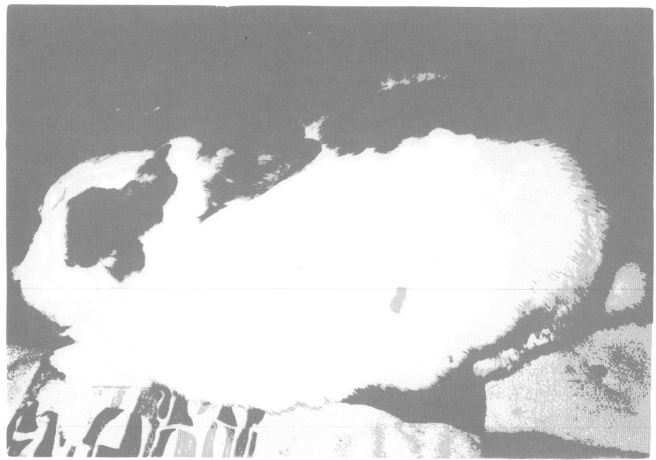

Step progression #3:
The negative was shot for
60 seconds. Color #3 was
printed on top of #1 and
#2 in a darker gray.

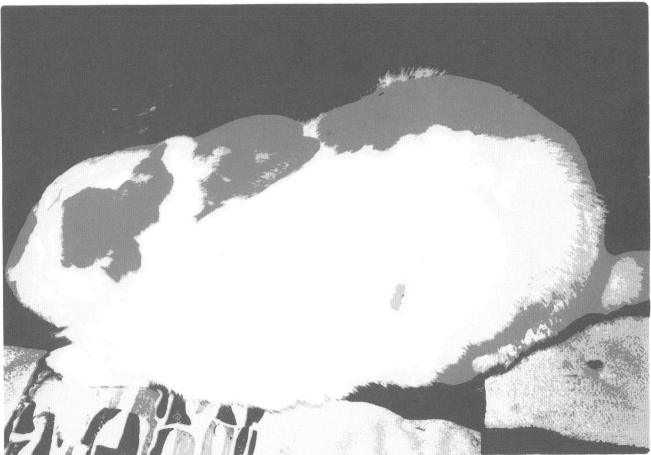

Step progression #4:
The negative was shot for
80 seconds. Color #4 was
printed in blue from the
positive.

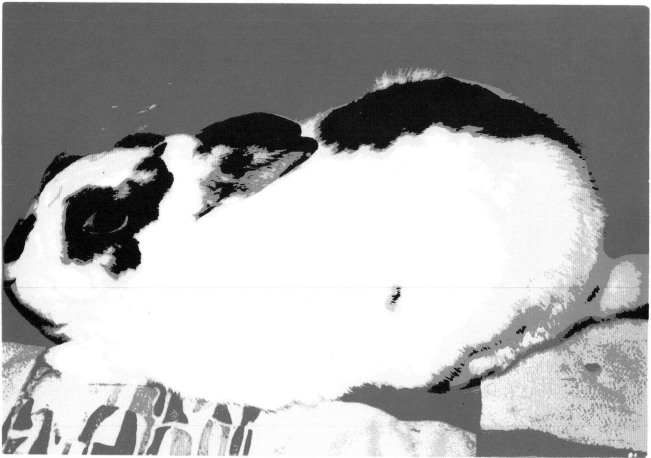

Step progression #5:
The negative was shot for
100 seconds. The positive
was printed in two colors, as
follows: The rabbit was printed
in black and then the stencil
was blocked out, and the
background was printed in
brown to complete the print
(opposite page).

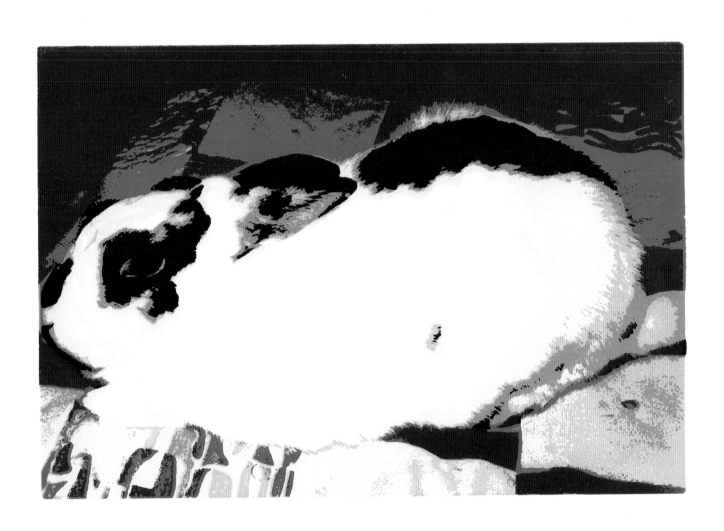

A small abstract painting by Dawn Henning-Santiago. This painting is analyzed and colors are made to match it.

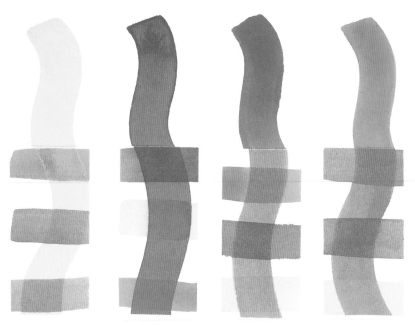

The four prominent watercolor colors that were matched to the abstract painting above. The series of color mixtures was made from the four colors being painted over each other.

Additional colors that could not be made with overlays: opaque gray and another shade of green.

THE LOGIC OF COLOR SEPARATIONS

Color photographs that are printed in magazines are made with a process called four-color separation. This is a mechanical method of copying the originals with a copy camera, using color filters, that produce four positive separations with dot patterns. These four represent the separate primary colors, yellow, magenta, and cyan, plus black. Using this system requires a very accurate knowledge of color reproduction, for a slight variation can ruin the results. Water-based ink prints four-color process very well, but the separations are made at specialized photo-stencil screenprinting shops to ensure accuracy. The mechanical process is used in combination with other separations, such as those done nonmechanically by the artist and/or printer.

The nonmechanical process requires an ability to decipher the number of colors, the order in which they were applied, and the style used to create them. Any piece of art can be made into color separations. I usually begin by looking for the most prominent colors. These are the colors that dominate the picture because of the amount of color, its contrast, or its intensity. For example, the abstract painting by Dawn Henning-Santiago shows that the most prominent colors come in this order:

1. Gray
2. Yellow
3. Green
4. Blue

The gray dominates the painting because of the amount of that color. The yellow and green, on the other hand, are the most intense. The blue covers a large amount also; it appears to go under the gray. Along with these four colors, there are many tints and shades. Instead of guessing what combinations of color there are, I make color swatches of the main four colors, matching them to the original. I mix up small amounts of those four colors using watercolor, which is faster and easier than using printing inks and screens. The printing inks can then be mixed to match the watercolors. The watercolor maintains its intensity even when it is transparent.

Next, I start making transparent overlays of all the colors over each other. The result of green, gray, and blue over yellow is, respectively, yellow-green, yellow-gray, and blue-green.

The result of gray, yellow, and green over blue is, respectively, gray-blue, olive blue, and deep green-blue.

I keep track of what color overlays another for reference when I make the separations. I need this information to determine the color order. I always cut out the swatches of the color mixtures and mount them in the correct color order. I mark how each was arrived at. Most of the colors in the original will be accounted for with this method. Any color that is not must be made as a separate color separation. This painting needs another gray and a brighter green to be made separately.

It is important to note that in deciding the number of colors there must be a limit, whether you are making a print for yourself or another artist. Even the most complicated originals that appear to have over one hundred colors can be translated into no more than thirty to forty color stencils.

Lynn Butler, *Haunted House*, 22 x 30" (56 x 76.2 cm). The four-color separations were made by E & A Screen Graphics. It was printed by Rand Russell in eight colors. The fabric was 265 orange monofilament, and it was printed with T.W. Graphics water-soluble halftone base and process colors.

Chapter 4

Preparing the Screen for Printing

The emulsion used to coat a screen is a photo emulsion—that is, it is light-sensitive. It is not as sensitive as photographic paper, which must be processed in a darkroom, but it still necessitates application under a yellow safelight. A stencil made of opaque material is placed in tight contact with a coated screen and exposed to ultraviolet light. The light hardens the emulsion wherever it is not masked off by the stencil. The emulsion remains soft in the masked-off areas, so that when the stencil is removed, the soft emulsion can washed away with water. The shapes of the opaque areas of the stencil wash away to become the open areas of the screen.

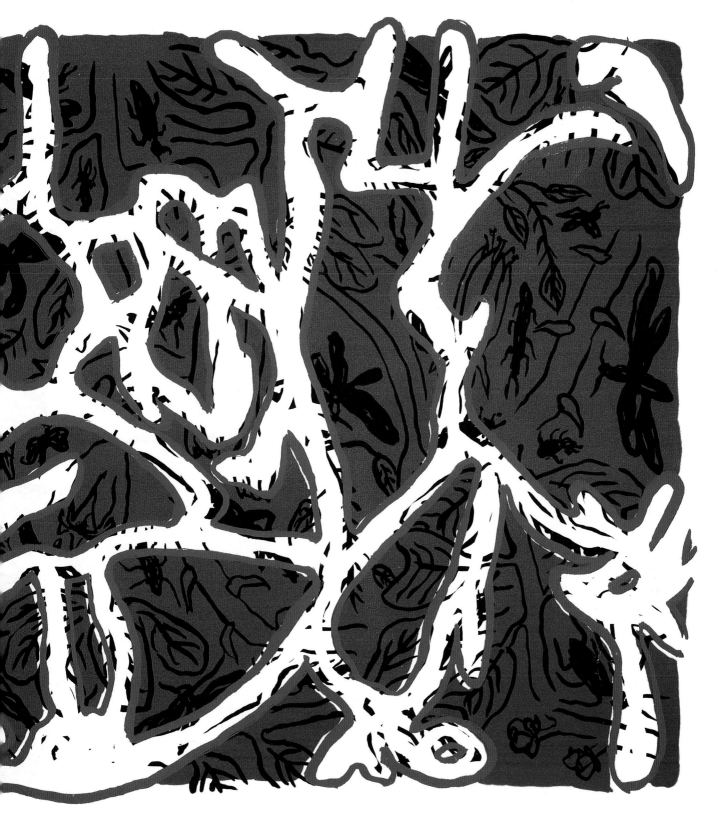

Kiki Smith, *Untitled*,
24 1/4 x 30" (56.5 x 76.2 cm).
This four-color print was shot
with an exposing unit that had
a built-in light source. It was
printed on Rives BFK gray paper
by the artist and Andrea Callard
in Lexington, New York, and
published by Avocet.

EMULSION APPLICATION

Using the photo emulsion, what you paint on a stencil is what will print; thus it is sometimes referred to as a photo-positive stencil. The exposure time is determined by the type of stencil, the number of coats of emulsion, and the light source.

MATERIALS

STRETCHED SCREEN
ABRASIVE CLEANSER
NYLON SCRUB BRUSH
WHITE VINEGAR
FAN OR HAIR DRYER
YELLOW SAFELIGHT
EMULSION
SCOOP COATER
SCOOP CARDS

Knife-cut, hand-drawn, painted, and photo stencils are all applied to the screen with direct photo emulsion. The screen must be degreased before it can be coated with emulsion. The degreasing enables the emulsion to flow evenly and smoothly over the screen during the application. Use any abrasive cleanser (such as Ajax or Comet) and a stiff nylon scrub brush. Wet the screen with water and sprinkle on the cleanser. Scrub it on both sides and wash it off with a hose. If it is degreased properly, water should flow smoothly, not bead up on the screen. Dry the screen thoroughly with a fan or hair dryer before

applying the emulsion. If the cleanser had bleach in it, neutralize the screen with an application of vinegar. Wash and dry it again before coating.

The emulsion scoop is designed to hold enough liquid emulsion to cover a screen with several even applications. Scoops come in different lengths and styles. All that is necessary is a smooth metal or rigid edge that can be pressed against the screen, a well to hold the emulsion, and a lip by which to hold the scoop with both hands.

Every screenprint supply company has several different light-sensitive emulsions to choose from. They all must be used under a yellow safelight. These lights are available at any photo supply store. Screen emulsions are water-soluble when in liquid form, and even after hardening they are removed with water and bleach or emulsion remover. For this reason, not all of them work well with water-based inks. Choosing an emulsion that specifically states on its label that it can be used with water-based inks is advisable.

Screen emulsions usually come in two parts: a liquid base and a sensitizer. They have a longer shelf-life before they are combined. Always follow the manufacturer's directions when mixing the emulsion. Some emulsions come with a dye to make them more visible on the screen. The delicately drawn, textured stencils used to make Tomar Levine's print *Jet Bead* (p. 74) were shot on screens single-coated with Ulano's 925-WR emulsion. It is very strong and can withstand the printing of large editions without breaking down. In breaking down, a stencil opens up in unwanted areas and allows the ink to print there.

Most photographic emulsions should be stored between 41° F and 95° F.

Coating the Screen

Prop the screen against a wall with the flat side facing out. Hammer two nails into the wall at the top of the screen and wedge the screen under the nails to prevent it from moving when you apply the emulsion. Once the screen is in place, pour the emulsion into the well of the scoop. Do not fill it to the top. Make sure that the scoop fits within the wooden frame and place it against the mesh at the bottom of the screen. Push

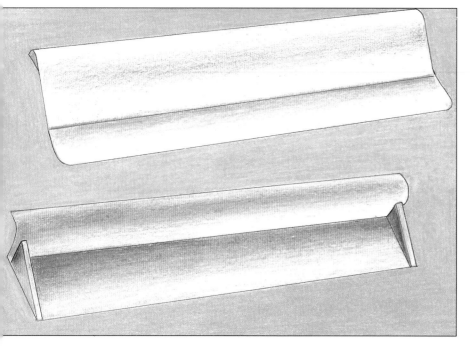

Two different styles of scoops for coating photo emulsion. One has sides that keep the emulsion from flowing out.

slightly into it—don't be afraid that you will hurt the mesh, for it is very strong. Resting only on the mesh, the scoop should be tilted towards the screen. Now grasp the lip evenly with both hands and while pushing firmly into the mesh, draw the emulsion up to the top of the screen. You should be able to see the emulsion fill the mesh as you move it from the bottom of the screen to the top. It should be all one color and thickness, without any lumps or streaks. At the top of the screen, tilt the scoop back toward you while keeping it firmly pressed against the screen. Then remove it. This prevents drips from the scoop getting on the screen.

If you are giving it a second coat, turn the screen over and apply it to the inside in exactly the same way. After the screen is coated, take a scoop card (cleanly cut pieces of cardboard or illustration board) and fill in the mesh on the sides of the screen with more emulsion. This is the area that the scoop could not reach. Usually there is an excess of emulsion on either side of the screen caused by the scoop as it moves from the bottom to the top. This excess can be used with the scoop card to fill in the open areas that were not reached on the first pass.

The screen mesh should be totally covered with emulsion when you are finished. Once the screen is coated, dry it thoroughly for at least two to three hours in front of a fan. A screen may be dried longer, even overnight, if it is stored in a dark, cool place. Drying the screen flat will produce the most even result. Follow the emulsion manufacturer's recommendations for the life of a coated screen.

Some printers prefer to coat a screen flat on a table or floor instead of leaning against a wall. Just make sure the screen is secure and will not move as it is coated; otherwise, your emulsion application can be ruined.

The number of coats of emulsion that you apply to a screen is determined by the stencil that is to be shot onto the screen. More coats make a thicker stencil, which prints a heavier deposit of ink which will then require a longer drying time. Fewer coats make a thinner stencil that will leave a finer deposit of ink on the paper.

COATING THE SCREEN:

The emulsion is poured into the well of the scoop coater. The screen is wedged against the wall so that it doesn't move during the application.

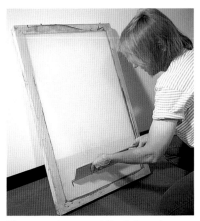

The scoop is pressed firmly into the mesh and slanted toward the screen.

The scoop is pulled up the screen and the emulsion is applied smoothly.

When the emulsion reaches the top, the scoop is slanted away from the screen to prevent it from dripping when it is removed.

A scoop card is used to fill in the open mesh with the excess emulsion.

EXPOSING THE SCREEN

Each manufacturer has a name for its own equipment. For example, Advance's exposure unit is called Polycop. Two other vacuum systems are made by and called Nu Arc and Phillington, and there are many others. They are all designed to hold a coated screen and a stencil in tight contact with each other, usually in a glass and steel case with a rubber blanket and a vacuum unit. The screen and stencil are placed inside. The rubber blanket lies over the screen, and the vacuum forces it to squeeze tightly around the screen. The unit swivels to an upright position so that the screen faces the light source.

MATERIALS

VACUUM FRAME EXPOSURE UNIT *OR*
VACUUM FRAME EXPOSURE UNIT
    WITH BUILT-IN LIGHT SOURCE *OR*
TABLE WITH FOAM RUBBER SQUARE
    AND PLATE GLASS
HALIDE LIGHT *OR*
PHOTOFLOOD LIGHT BULB AND REFLECTOR
WASHOUT STAND

There are direct-contact exposure units that have a built-in light source and a similar vacuum frame. The screen and stencil are placed on a glass case that houses a number of ultraviolet tube lights. When the frame is closed over the screen, the rubber blanket tightens over it and the lights are turned on. The advantage of this system is that it is self-contained.

In lieu of the built-in ultraviolet lights, a metal halide light system is a good choice for exposing screens. It is available in different watt units and comes with a stand or an overhead mounting bracket.

When the lamp is turned on, the light is hidden behind a shutter that is operated by a timer. The lamp becomes very hot, so it is kept cool with a built-in fan. When the screen is placed in a vacuum frame exposing unit, the halide lamp is set up in front of it, at a distance that varies according to the stencil being exposed. A good rule is to measure the art (stencil) diagonally and place the lamp at that distance away from it. The timer is set for the length of the exposure, and the on button is pushed. The shutter will open, expose the screen, and close. The lamp is turned off only after everything that has to be exposed is shot. Once the lamp is turned completely off, it must cool down before it can be turned on again. This light can expose a screen in as short a time as twelve seconds.

A Homemade Exposing Unit

A photoflood light, found at a photo supply store or screen supply company, can be placed in an aluminum reflector and suspended over a table for a homemade unit. Cover the table with a piece of foam rubber two inches thick. The table top should be smaller than the coated screen—that is, the frame of the screen should hang over the top on all four sides. The stencil is taped to the back of the screen and a piece of plate glass 1/4 inch to 1/2 inch thick is placed over it. The weight of the glass makes the contact between the screen and the stencil very tight. It is always your objective to get the contact very tight. This is a simple and inexpensive method of shooting a screen when a vacuum frame exposure unit is unavailable.

EXPOSURE PROCEDURE

Once the screen is coated and has dried for at least two hours, tape the stencil securely to the back or flat side of the screen with clear tape. Make sure there is enough space around the stencil so that your squeegee fits across it with at least three inches to spare on each side (more space is even better). The stencil is placed backward on the flat side so that it reads correctly when you look into the screen on the squeegee side.

Place the screen with the taped stencil onto the glass of the exposure unit. The flat side with the stencil should lie on the glass. Close the vacuum frame and make sure it is in very tight contact. Turn on the vacuum switch and wait for the rubber blanket to suck tightly around the frame of the screen. When all the air has been exhausted, swivel the unit to a vertical position facing the light source. The flat side of the screen will be facing the light, and the stencil will be backward.

The rule of thumb for exposing a screen is: shorter time for detail, and longer time for solid shapes. The longer you expose a screen, the greater the

Opposite page:
James Rizzi, *That's Amori*, 29 1/2 x 22" (75 x 56 cm). The print was made with screens that were double-coated with Stencoat direct emulsion, made by T.W. Graphics, and exposed for thirty seconds under a halide lamp. It was printed by the author and Greg Radich at the Screenprint Workshop. Rizzi's print is later cut out and assembled into a three-dimensional print. Published by John Szoke, New York.

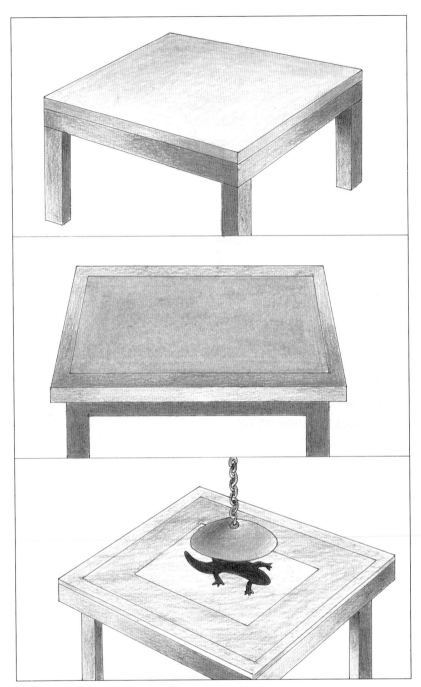

Top: A simple table with a two-inch piece of foam rubber covering the top.

Center: A screen is placed over the foam rubber with the frame hanging over the edge of the table. A stencil is taped to the back, facing up.

Bottom: Plate glass is used to make a tight contact between the coated screen and the stencil. A photoflood light in an aluminum reflector is suspended overhead.

chance that light will seep in around the edges of stenciled shapes. This would shrink the areas which should print, and details would be lost (less of the emulsion where details appear would remain soft and wash away, leaving open mesh). Of course, with too short an exposure, emulsion will not harden properly and will wash away.

A shorter exposure time must be combined with fewer coats of emulsion. A longer exposure time must be combined with more coats of emulsion.

A long or short exposure time is also determined by the light source. A short exposure with a halide light could be ten to fifteen seconds. A short exposure with a photoflood could be ten minutes.

Most companies make recommendations for the use of their emulsions. It is always a good idea to begin there and to test emulsion coatings with different exposure times. To make a test, coat sections of a screen with different amounts in a range of one to six. Then expose the same stencil using the same light source. Do this several times to allow for different exposures. Keep a record for comparisons. When the screen is washed, the open mesh will be different for each coated section. Compare it to the stencil and see which time and coating give the best result.

SCREEN WASHOUT

For beginners with small screens, the washing of the screen can be done simply in a bathtub with a spray nozzle hose attachment. Professional shops use metal washout stands that resemble huge troughs with a high back and sides and a low front. This comes with a drain and hose attachment. Fancy ones have a built-in light source to backlight the screen, which allows you to inspect the emulsion washout more closely.

MATERIALS

WASHOUT STAND
SPRAY WATER BOTTLE
HOSE WITH NOZZLE
FAN

Once the screen exposure has been done, remove the screen from the vacuum frame. This must all be done under yellow safelights. Take off the stencil and save it for registration later.

EXPOSING THE SCREEN:

Clear tape is used to attach the stencil (here, a crayon drawing on textured acetate) to the back of the screen. The stencil should look correct when you look into the screen from the inside, or printing side.

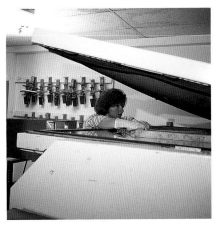

A Polycop vacuum exposing unit. The screen is shown on the glass with the flat side down before the frame is closed.

The vacuum frame is swiveled to a vertical position facing the halide light.

A halide ultraviolet light for exposing screens. The shutter is closed over the light.

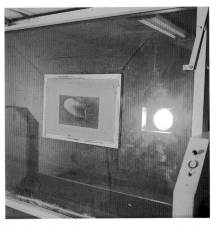

The timer has been turned on, opening the shutter and exposing the screen and stencil in the vacuum frame. The bluishness is caused by the ultraviolet light.

Once the screen is shot, it is removed from the vacuum frame. This crayon drawing was shot for twenty-five seconds.

APPROXIMATE EXPOSURE TIMES

INK RESULT	STENCIL	EMULSION	LIGHT	EXPOSURE
1. Opaque, heavy deposit	Hard-edged, solid	2 or more coats	Halide	30 or more seconds
2. Thin, transparent color	Fine detail, crayon or halftone	1 coat	Halide	10–20 seconds
3. Opaque, heavy deposit	Hard-edged, solid	2 or more coats	Photoflood	20–30 minutes
4. Thin, transparent color	Fine detail, crayon or halftone	1 or 2 coats	Photoflood	10–15 minutes

Tomar Levin, *Jet Bead*,
34 x 28¼" (86.3 x 71.7 cm).
Hand-drawn on textured acetate,
the stencils were shot on screens
coated with Ulano's 925-WR
emulsion. The time exposure was
twenty-two seconds. Published by
Orion Editions, New York.

Put the screen in the washout stand with the flat side facing out. Using a lukewarm spray, wet the back of the screen. This should be a fine spray, nothing harsh. Turn the screen over to the front side and spray it also. The image of the stencil should start to appear. Turn it over again to the back side and continue spraying. The emulsion will continue to wash out, and the open screen mesh should be visible.

Without some experience, it is very difficult to see if the emulsion has washed out completely. If it looks clean, if no more emulsion is washing out, and if the surface of the screen is no longer slimy to the touch, it is probably washed enough. Hold the screen up to the yellow light. You should be able to see if there is a thin residue of emulsion left in the stencil area of the screen. You will be able to look through the mesh at the light if it is cleanly washed out and compare it to the stencil it was exposed to. If it doesn't compare, continue washing.

When you are finished, lightly wash the screen with cold water and place it in front of a fan to dry. This is a standard method for coating and exposing screens. But once you understand the principle, you can push the method to allow for more and more complex results.

Alternative Washout for Water Conservation

Screens can also be washed out with warm water, a sponge, and a spray bottle. Wet the screen with a sponge and warm water. Keep a bucket of water to dip the sponge in and an empty bucket to squeeze the dirty sponge into. Do this until the image begins to appear. Make sure to wash both sides of the screen. Using the water bottle, spray directly into the stencil area of the screen until the emulsion washes out. Make sure, as with the other method, that you wash the screen enough. It must not feel slimy to the touch. This method not only conserves water, but gives you better control over special and detailed areas of the screen.

A unique system for holding the softest washes painted on textured acetate has been developed by Rand

SCREEN WASHOUT:

After exposure, the screen is placed in a washout stand with the flat side facing out. The image begins to appear as the screen is washed with a hose and a warm water spray.

This is an alternative washout method that will conserve water. A spray water bottle is used, so the amount of water is more easily controlled.

The screen is held up to the light to see if all the emulsion has washed out.

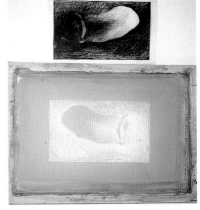

Comparing the stencil drawing to the washed screen. The flat side of the screen faces out, so it shows the reverse of the drawing. The drawing looks correct on the inside, or printing side, of the screen.

After the screen is dry, it is looked at with a light behind it. This helps you to see any pinholes. These are touched up with emulsion and a brush.

This close-up of the screen shows the artist touching up the flaws. The emulsion is on the dark areas, and the open mesh is the light area.

These two progressive proofs made by Rand Russell using her unique exposure and washout system have the look of a watercolor wash. They were printed with transparent Createx Lyntex base and pigment. The stencils were textured Lexan painted by the artist Mariella Bisson in translucent washes using speed opaque.

Mariella Bisson, *Boulder Ridge, Prospect Park*, 30 x 22" (76.2 x 56 cm). The finished print has three colors, the last a darker gray that simulates a charcoal drawing. It was printed and published by Rand Russell.

Russell, an artist and master printer. Usually, when paint is applied to textured acetate (or Lexan), only the most opaque parts translate to the screen during exposure; translucent areas drop out. Most printers rely on halftone dots, crayon, or mezzotints to copy these areas. Ms. Russell, through experimentation, developed a method of exposing screens that holds the translucent washes. Using Ulano's 925-WR emulsion, she double-coats a screen stretched with 230 orange monofilament. She puts one coat on the back and one on the front and dries it flat. This much is standard procedure. The departure is with her light source. She uses a movie-set light that emits a smaller amount of ultraviolet. The exposure time is nine to ten minutes. With my halide light, this would be an overexposure, and my emulsion would not wash out. But with her light, it is actually an underexposure. This is considered a slow cure.

When the screen is washed with cold water, most of the emulsion washes away, as in the case of an underexposed screen. What is left behind is the open-mesh area where the opaque paint was and a very fine, nearly filled-in area where the translucent paint was. The emulsion is very thin here, with only the tiniest holes. The screen is so tightly bonded with this emulsion that Russell doesn't bother to reclaim them. The printed result is the closest I've seen to a lithographic wash. The Mariella Bisson print illustrated here shows just how delicate such screenprinting can be.

Problems to Look for

The screen will break down and open up in unwanted areas as a result of one or more of the following:

> Too vigorous washing, especially with water that is too hot.
> Underexposure.
> The emulsion is uneven or too thick.
> The emulsion is too old.

The screen will not wash out in the stencil areas because of:

> Underwashing.
> Too long an exposure.
> Too thin a coat of emulsion.
> An emulsion that is too old.

Sometimes a very thin amount of emulsion will not be noticed in the open mesh of the screen. This will block the passage of the ink and will show up when you try to print a color. Spray it with water on the printing table. If it doesn't come out, reshoot the screen.

THE FINAL TOUCH-UP

When the screen is dry, remove it to a room with white light and look for pinholes. Best seen when looking into the screen with the light behind it, these show up as minuscule points of light in the emulsion. Bits of dust in the vacuum frame act as opaque material and block the emulsion from hardening; when the screen is washed, these tiny holes open up. If not closed, they will print as spots.

With a brush or a scoop card and some emulsion, touch up all the areas on the screen where this occurs. This is the point at which all corrections to the screen are made before printing. Dry the screen one more time with a fan or hair dryer. Place the screen in front of your light and harden it again. I usually reharden a screen for five minutes in front of a halide light. This ensures that the stencil will hold up firmly under the pressure of printing.

OIL-BASED VS. WATER-BASED PREPARATION

There are, of course, a number of differences between screen preparations for oil-based printing and for water-based printing. The following recommendations are therefore offered assuming that you have elected to print with water-based inks.

First, in the choice of emulsion, make sure it is recommended for use with water-based ink.

After the screen is exposed, it must be hardened again. This is not always necessary with the emulsions used with oil-based ink.

Emulsion is used to touch up and block out the screen. Companies are beginning to make screen fillers for water-based work, such as Hunt Speedball screen filler. With oil-based inks you would still use water-soluble block-outs to touch up screens.

Always follow the manufacturer's recommendations when using a photo emulsion. It is still considered a toxic substance and contains diazo, a harmful chemical. Wearing gloves is advisable.

Chapter 5

Water-Based Ink

For years, screenprinting ink manufacturers concentrated on perfecting and inventing better surfaces, faster evaporations, and durability with their oil-based technology. Water-based ink was relegated to textile printing and crafts. The choices for a serious artist or printmaker were few. Today, because of the increased demand for a safer, less toxic ink, manufacturers have created water-based inks that meet all the requirements for high-quality, fine-art editions with good resolution. In this chapter, I discuss just a sampling of the growing number of excellent inks that I have used or tested.

David Grubb,
Saddle Creek, Evening,
29 3/4 x 37 1/2" (75.5 x 95.2 cm).
Printed by Jim Roche.

Colors made with Hunt's Speedball water-based ink.

Gladys Burrows, *Red Poles*, 11¹/₂ x 15¹/₄" (29.2 x 38.7 cm). Printed by the author at the Screenprint Workshop with Hunt's water-based inks.

DIFFERENT BRANDS

Most manufacturers now have a water-based line of inks. Some, like Colonial Inks, plan to introduce one in a year. As with the majority of printmakers, I use one or two brands that fit my needs, but I have examined brands that are used by other printmakers and been given samples of their editions. Generally, the overall quality of the inks is similar. The degree of toxicity between the brands does differ, and it is up to the individual artist or printer to familiarize him- or herself with the differences and to make a choice. When you are uncertain, speak to the chemists and technicians at the various companies. They are very helpful, and each manufacturer will supply a materials safety data sheet.

Hunt's Speedball Water-Soluble Screenprinting Ink

These inks are available in a full range of colors and of bases to make the colors transparent. The chemist at Hunt Manu-

facturing Company was available to answer any questions concerning the ink. Years ago, I had tried their products and found the ink inferior for use with fine-art editioning. Recently, however, I gave them another try, found them to be improved, and started using them. Mr. Al Spizzo, a chemist at Hunt, explained that the ink had been reformulated, and I agreed with him that it is now a much better product.

This ink has the added advantage of being tested by the Arts and Crafts Materials Institute in Boston and issued an AP (approved product) nontoxic seal by that group. Not all brands have this specific seal.

Hunt's colors tend to be more transparent than oil-based ink, and the consistency is quite thick. I found the ink easy to print with. The print *Red Poles*, by Gladys Burrows, was printed with Hunt's water-based ink in an edition of 300 with a mezzotint screen and ten additional colors.

Createx Pure Pigment and Lyntex Base

Createx pigments and base have been tested by me but not used for fine-art editions. However, they are used by many fine printmakers and printers, including Lynwood Kreneck, Andrea Callard, and Rand Russell, with excellent results.

Createx makes pure pigments that are nontoxic, concentrated colors combined with Lyntex base (named after Professor Lynwood Kreneck, of Texas Tech University's Art Department, the formulator of this water-based medium for printing on paper). The result is a transparent screenprinting color. It is combined with gouache medium or titanium white to make it opaque. These pigments are available in a wide range of colors, including pearlescent colors, which have a metallic sheen.

Createx pigments have also been tested by the Arts and Crafts Materials Institute and found to be nontoxic and permanent. They have been given a CP (certified product) seal of approval. These products also come with a materials safety data sheet. I find their inks more transparent than oil-based inks. The consistency is very similar to Hunt's water-based ink. Andrea Callard has

printed with Createx pigments and Lyntex base extensively and has gotten very good results. Her edition of *Mind and Body/Getting Well*, by Gail Nathan, is evidence of this.

T.W. Graphics

T.W. Graphics Screen Process Supply manufactures not only ink but also equipment, and it offers screenprinting services. Most of their ink is solvent-based, but they also have a very good line of water-based ink. I have tested this ink and have made fine-art editions with it for many years. It has improved over time, and many heavy metals have been eliminated from it. The ink is opaque, and bases are available to make it transparent. It has a looser consistency than oil-based ink, but the coverage and opacity are the same. Their WB-1000 series dries with a matte finish, and the WB-2000 series is glossy. These inks can be used to print on many surfaces besides paper.

T.W. Graphics also has a halftone base for printing fine photographic detail. When I originally tried this product, the ink took a long time to dry thoroughly when there were many layers of ink. If you picked a print from

Gail Nathan,
Mind and Body/Getting Well,
22 x 30" (56 x 76.2 cm).
For this edition of thirty, the ink was Createx pure pigments used with Lyntex base. There were eight colors and a color blend. The print was published by Avocet.

Mixtures of Createx pure pigments and Lyntex base.

Top: Elsie Manville, *Legendary Lovers*,
26 x 37" (66 x 94 cm). This thirty-five-color print
was printed at the Screenprint Workshop by the
author and Greg Radich with T.W. Graphics 1000
series water-based ink. All the separations were hand-
drawn on textured acetate by Elsie Manville and the
author. Published by Orion Editions, New York.

Above: David A. Dunlop, *Water Lights*,
26 x 53³/₄" (66 x 136.5 cm).
The stencils for this eighteen-color print were made
by the artist with black acrylic paint on textured
acetate. It was printed with T.W. Graphics' water-
based ink by the author and Greg Radich.
Published by Orion Editions, New York.

T.W. Graphics water-based 1000 series.

the stack of editions, you could hear a swish sound, and the print would release slowly from the one underneath. There was no damage, but it was unnerving. This problem has been resolved by the company.

A company representative is always available to discuss the inks and their contents. I have printed both opaque and transparent prints using T.W. Graphics inks, with excellent results.

The multicolored prints of Elsie Manville (*Legendary Lovers*) and David Dunlop (*Water Lights*) were printed with T.W. Graphics water-based 1000 series.

Union Inks

The Union Ink Company is also a large manufacturer that has produced some of the best oil-based ink. Today they also have a very fine series of water-based inks called Echo Print WFPR,

Union Ink's color swatches.

Ross Blechner,
Campaign for Military Service,
25 x 38" (63.5 x 96.5 cm).
Union Ink Company's Echo water-based series was used by Jean-Yves Noblet, of Noblet Serigraphic, Inc., New York, to print this work of eleven colors.

Paul Laster, *Endless Voyage*, 20 x 26" (50.8 x 66 cm). Printed with Union's water-based ink at Noblet Serigraphic, Inc. The 85-line halftone was printed with 305 monofilament.

Inks made from Lascaux Screenprinting Paste.

which can be printed on paper. The ink dries with a matte look and is probably the closest in appearance to oil-based ink. The consistency is very thick, and the opacity is excellent. Although I have not done fine-art editioning with it, Jean-Yves Noblet, of Noblet Serigraphic, Inc., uses it exclusively. He has printed many editions that required very delicate texture and fine meshes for airbrush stencils without a problem, and his results are excellent. The print *Campaign for Military Service*, by Ross Blechner (p. 83), was printed with Union inks, and the halftone screen used to print an edition for Paul Laster (above) was shot on 305 mono-filament and printed with Union inks.

Lascaux Screenprinting Paste
Lascaux, long known for its excellent colors, has developed a screenprinting paste that can be mixed with its acrylics to make a screenprinting ink. Recently introduced in this country, it has been used in Europe with very good results.

The screenprinting paste is a clear, concentrated gel made from acrylic resin and glycol. It produces an ink which does not run on the screen, but stays in gel form until it is pushed through the mesh. It is a system similar to that of Createx, which also employs squeeze bottles to hold the pigments and then mix with the base. Lascaux still uses cadmium and cobalts in their acrylics; these are toxic.

VARIETY AMONG INKS
Variety among inks derives from surface quality (matte or gloss), the intensity of color (added pigments and concentrates), and the transparency or opacity.

In the case of oil-based inks, the variety is consistent with every brand. With water-based inks, there are variations from brand to brand. Inks like Createx or even Lascaux derive their variety from the colors that are mixed with the screenprinting base. For some brands, there may not be a gloss series of inks available, as there is in oil-based inks, though the range of colors can still be complex, depending upon the number of pigments available. For example, Hunt's ink only has a matte finish. Gloss is obtained with a gloss overprint varnish. This is printed at the end of an edition to make the prints shiny. (Hunt's will be introducing a series of gloss inks in the near future.) T.W. Graphics has a more complete variety of water-based inks. Their 1000 series offers a matte finish, and the 2000 series is glossy. They also have a 3000 series of water-based baking enamels; I have never tried these.

In addition to their color choices, T.W. Graphics offers a large number of color concentrates, or toners, to add to the inks to intensify the color. I have added watercolor or gouache to water-based ink to intensify the color.

Transparent base is available in all the brands named above. Transparency is created by adding transparent base to ink or pigment. The more base, the greater the transparency. There are also halftone bases formulated to print photographic dot patterns.

Metallic Powders

Metallic powders can be added to transparent base to print metallic colors. They must be handled very carefully while wearing a mask to guard against inhaling the powder. The print by Richard Mock, *Man Perceiving* (p. 86), was printed with aluminum powder and transparent base.

RETARDERS

Retarders are added to ink for two reasons: (1) to improve the result that occurs when it prints by acting as a flow agent, which makes the ink more printable through the mesh of the screen; and (2) to retard evaporation and thereby prevent the ink from drying in the screen. Water-based ink is difficult to remove from the screen once it is allowed to dry. Some of the brands listed only recommend water to thin the ink and keep it printable. Others have retarders that are sold specifically for that purpose. I use mostly water and occasionally Golden's retarder, sold as a part of the Golden Artist Colors line of acrylic paints. Union Inks puts out its own retarder, as does T.W. Graphics. Printer Jean-Yves Noblet uses a retarder from International Chemical Company to add to Union Ink. He claims that he never has a problem with the ink drying.

COLOR MIXING AND MATCHING

Mixing colors with water-based ink is easy. The colors are comparable to oil-based ink, and washing up is simple. You just use water. Follow all the same rules that are used in mixing any colors you paint with. The three primary colors are red, yellow, and blue. The secondary colors are orange, green, and purple; and the tertiary colors are the colors between these colors on the color wheel. These, combined with white and black, will give you a full palette.

It would be unrealistic in the space of this chapter to try to teach someone who has never worked with color how to mix colors for screenprinting. If you are a beginner, I recommend that you begin with a set of acrylic paints and experiment before trying large amounts of screen ink. But for those artists and printers with some familiarity with color, here are a few tips:

1. Test the opacity (that is, the solid coverage of the ink that prevents the color underneath from showing through) by making a small rectangle stencil on a screen to print with. Usually, but not always, the reds and yellows are more transparent than the darker colors, regardless of the brand (this includes oil-based ink). Adding white will usually make a color more opaque, though of course it also lightens and lessens the intensity of the color.

2. To make a color transparent, always start with the transparent base and slowly add the pigment. Otherwise, you will end up with a lot more ink than you need.

3. To mix a light color, the same thing applies. Start with white and then add the pigment. For example, when mixing a pink you would start with white and add red.

4. It is also important to know that inks dry lighter or darker depending on the color and the brand.

OPAQUE

TRANSLUCENT

TRANSPARENT

This is a sample of opaque, translucent, and transparent colors.

Color Proofing

Proofing a color is a natural extension of mixing a color. Proofing means taking the color you have mixed and printing it through a small area (like a square or rectangle) on a screen, drying it with a hair dryer, and comparing it to the original (if there is one).

If there is no original and you are proofing to see if you like a color, it is still necessary to dry it to see the true color. When a color swatch is dry, cut it out with scissors or a mat knife, removing the white paper, and then compare it to the color that you want to match. Otherwise, the white paper interferes; you cannot judge the true color of the swatch.

Matching a Color

Matching colors is an acquired skill that is the result of mixing and proofing many colors. There are systems that can be followed, like the Pantone Matching System (often referred to as PMS colors), but I have found practice and observation are the best methods. Obviously, we look at and choose colors all the time, such as when we select our clothes. Blue pants come in light and dark shades. They look blue, but may also be a greenish blue. It is the same with matching colors.

Look at the color you want to match—let's say it is a blue. With every brand of ink, color swatches are available. Compare the blue you want to match with these swatches. Perhaps there are three different blues to choose from. Pick the closest to the original color you want to match and begin there. Now evaluate how much darker or lighter the blue swatch is from your blue. This is the *value* of that color. Check the intensity, or brightness, of the blue: Is it lighter, but still bright, or is it lighter and duller? Proceed from there. If the original blue is lighter and duller, you may just add white, but if it is lighter and still a bright greenish-blue, you will have to make it light but keep that intensity by adding a light color, a green or perhaps a yellow.

This can be a slow process, and many swatches of color must be printed to get a good match. Mix small amounts each time you change a color. This will keep you from overmixing.

David Grubb compares a color swatch with the original painting during the proofing of *Hybrid Pink*.

Opposite page:
Richard Mock, *Man Perceiving*, 30 x 22" (76.2 x 56 cm). This small edition of twenty was printed by Andrea Callard and the artist, using aluminum powder mixed with water-soluble transparent base. Published by Avocet.

Once the colors are mixed and matched, the print is proofed to see if the color order is correct. A set of progressive proofs for David Grubb's print *Hybrid Pink* is shown in Chapter 6.

OIL-BASED VS. WATER-BASED INK

The first difference to be noted, of course, is the lack of solvents in the use of water-based inks, and the easy cleanup. However, there is less variety with water-based ink. This is easily compensated for by a wonderful surface quality. First, the water-based matte surface does not scuff as easily as the oil-based matte is prone to do. The latter tends to be very fragile. Second, when a water-based color is proofed over another color and you don't like it, it can be washed off with a sponge and water and printed again. This certainly saves on proofs.

My experience printing with these inks for the last six years has been very good. I had printed with oil-based products for twelve years prior to my switch. The water-based inks make beautiful professional prints, and in these and other ways they are superior.

Chapter 6

Printing the Image

To do screenprinting, your choice of apparatus depends on the size and complexity of the images to be printed. A manufactured table with a vacuum for holding the paper would be ideal, but prints have been made on any flat surface with a good means of securing the screen. A drying rack is essential, and a squeegee with a sharp blade will ensure success. Beyond the choice of good equipment and supplies is the necessity of working in an orderly, methodical way. This chapter provides a number of helpful tips on how to tend effectively to the details of the printing process.

James Rizzi,
The City That Never Sleeps,
22 x 29¹/₂" (56 x 75 cm).
Printed by the author and
Greg Radich, this work is cut
and assembled into a 3-D
image. Published by John
Szoke.

Two different styles of hinge clamps. Both are made of heavy, durable metal with a compartment that fits and tightens over the frame of a screen and a piece that screws into the table.

A simple wooden table with huge clamps.

A compartment with a vacuum hose attachment.

This table with screen has a vacuum compartment built under the table.

PREPARING A TABLE

Any sturdy wooden table that has a flat surface can be utilized for printing. Formica, purchased at any home repair or lumber center, can be glued to the table top to provide a smooth surface that is easily cleaned with soap and water. Screw two hinge clamps, obtained at any screenprinting supply store, to the back of the table at either end in line with each other. These allow the screen to lift up and down from the front of the table while the back remains attached.

MATERIALS

PRINTING TABLE
MOVABLE TABLE FOR PAPER
DRYING RACK
SQUEEGEE
INK AND CONTAINERS
SPATULA
MASKING TAPE
CELLOPHANE TAPE
PAPER TOWELS
PIECES OF CARDBOARD OR
    ILLUSTRATION BOARD
WATER SPRAY BOTTLE
PAPER

Vacuum Suction Device

Professional printing tables have a vacuum that holds the paper down and keeps it from moving during printing. A simple vacuum system can be made for the wooden table using a vacuum cleaner and hose. Build a shallow wooden compartment under the table-top. Drill holes through the wood and formica of the tabletop, one hole per inch. Cut an opening in the wooden compartment that will accommodate the vacuum hose. Nail the compartment to the underside of the tabletop and seal the seams with glue or duct tape. This will make it airtight. When the vacuum is turned on, it will suck air down through the holes into the compartment. This will hold your paper down and prevent it from moving. This is important to maintain good registration.

Professional printers use a metal vacuum table with a one-arm squeegee attachment. Some tables have an automatic blow-back vacuum system that holds the paper when the screen is down and releases the paper when the screen is up. Other tables have vacuums that are operated manually by the printers after each printing.

The one-arm squeegee is a unit that consists of a bar with a handle that the squeegee fits into. This assembly glides perpendicular to the back of the table on ball bearings. The screen is attached to the back supports of the system with chains that are clamped onto the front of the screen frame on two sides. This table also comes equipped with a screen clamp bar at the back of the table and a counterbalance assembly that permits the screen to raise and lower easily. When the printer lifts the screen, the counterbalance maintains it in the up position.

Movable Table for Paper

The paper must be kept close to the printing table for easy access. Use an existing drawing table and add casters to the feet so that it will move readily. A simple wooden table can be made with 2 x 4" pieces of pine. Choose a size that will accommodate many different sizes of papers.

A simple construction for making a table would call for twelve pieces of 2 x 4" wood and two pieces of 3/4" plywood for the top and one shelf. The lengths of the 2 x 4's would depend on the size you wanted to build. Nail the 2 x 4's together in a box construction using common nails and epoxy (see illustration). Cut the plywood to fit the top and the shelf on the bottom. It can be cut at the lumber company once you determine the size. Put one set of four casters on the bottom.

DRYING RACKS

Each sheet of paper that is printed must be placed on a rack to dry. Professional drying racks are made of metal criss-crossed wire shelves that permit air to circulate around the prints and dry very quickly. Each shelf is attached to the back of a metal frame with an adjustable spring that holds it in place when it is moved up or down. These racks are available in various sizes with fifty shelves to a rack.

When a professional metal drying rack is unavailable, a simple version can be made. Measure your printing paper. The shelves of the rack should be larger

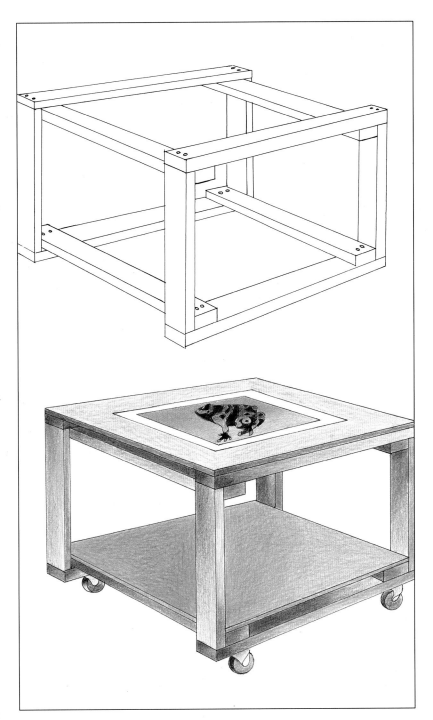

Top: A box-frame construction for a movable table to hold the paper supply.

Bottom: The movable table with the top and casters attached.

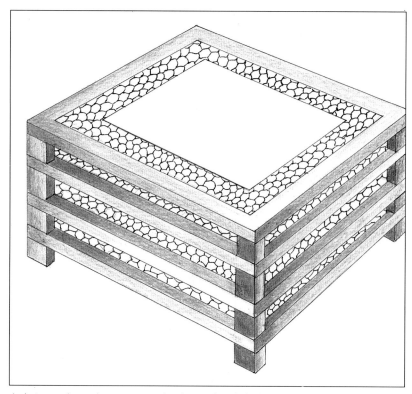

A drying rack can be constructed with wood and chicken wire. Pegs hold the shelves apart.

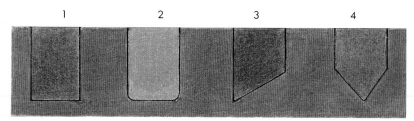

There are several different squeegee blades:
(1) for printing on paper,
(2) for printing heavy ink deposits,
(3) for printing on glass,
(4) for printing on uneven surfaces.

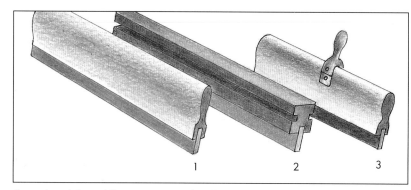

Examples of three different squeegee handles:
(1) hand squeegee,
(2) one-arm squeegee,
(3) hand squeegee with a grip.

than the paper size. Build a wooden frame out of 1" slat wood (if the paper is very heavy, use stronger wood for the frame). Nail and glue the end joints. Now cover this frame with a wire screening such as chicken wire. There are many different kinds of screening available at lumber companies and home repair centers. Chicken wire is one of the cheapest. Again, the weight and thickness of the wire is determined by the size and weight of the paper. Buy enough wire to cover the number of shelves needed to accommodate the number of sheets of paper to be printed. I would not exceed thirty frames, for it starts to get costly, and you can reuse racks as the prints dry.

Measure and cut the wire with wire cutters so that it fits over the frame. Staple each cut piece of chicken wire to each frame. Cover the wire over the frame with duct tape; it's cut edges are sharp. Nail pegs on all four corners of each frame to separate the shelves and allow air to circulate. Either cut 2" pieces of wood from another 1 x 2" length to make pegs, or buy pegs at the lumberyard.

Before a color is printed, simply place one of the shelves on the floor. Print a color and put that sheet on the shelf. Stack another shelf on top of it. As each color is printed, the paper is placed on a shelf and another shelf is stacked on top of it.

SQUEEGEES

Squeegees are used to print the colors. They push the ink through the open mesh of the screen onto the paper. They consist of two parts: a blade and a wooden handle. The blade is inserted into a groove in the handle and screwed or clamped in place. Squeegees come in different compositions, sizes, styles, or durometers.

The composition of the blade is either rubber or plastic. The standard is rubber, used mostly by students, and it is the least expensive. Rubber wears down faster with use than plastic does, and since a sharp edge determines the quality of the printed ink on paper, this is a very important point. Solvent-based inks wear the rubber down even faster.

The *durometer* is the hardness or softness of the blade and is equally important. A softer blade requires less pressure, so it works best with small hand squeegees. A medium durometer, preferably plastic, is good with a one-arm squeegee, which affords more pressure and requires less flexibility.

To restore the sharp edge of the blade once it has worn down after many printings, it can be sanded. Staple a length of fine sandpaper to a wooden board for stability. Rub the squeegee back and forth across the sandpaper to restore the edge. Use steel wool after the sanding to make it smooth again. If the printed color has streaks from the sanding, rub the blade with more steel wool until the color prints uniformly.

There are also a number of different blade shapes and squeegee handles. The common squeegee blade for printing fine-art editions on paper is flat with two sharp edges. Squeegees come in many lengths, from a few inches to several feet, and they can be purchased in a standard size or made to order.

The squeegee should fit easily within the frame of the screen, but also two to three inches over the open stencil on either side.

It is advisable to tape the squeegee to prevent ink from seeping up into the groove where the blade fits into the handle. Use masking or duct tape. This will also make the squeegee easier to clean. This is most important in using oil-based inks, because their solvents keep dissolving the ink buildup in the groove. Streaks of different colors from previous printings will then drip down and show up in the new color being printed. When water-based ink dries in the handle of the squeegee, it does not redissolve from water, thereby lessening the chance of this happening. The main reason for taping in this case is to help with the cleanup.

KNOWING YOUR PAPERS
Water-based ink, like oil-based, prints on almost any paper surface. Paper comes in many different forms and surfaces—smooth, rough, hard, soft, coated, and porous. Each will give a different result.

Paper is made several ways: handmade, mold-made, and machine-made.

Handmade paper is very beautiful, but it is usually expensive, being made in small quantities. Quality varies with each sheet. It is also very absorbent and comes with a *deckle* on all four sides—a ragged or rough edge that is formed as a result of the papermaking process. The edge takes its name from the wooden frame-like device that fits over the outer edges of the mold that contains the water and fibers for making the paper. During this process some fibers slip under the wooden deckle and cause the rough, or deckle, edge.

Mold-made paper is more consistent, but it resembles handmade paper and is also beautiful. The grain of the paper has a definite direction. It is made with a cylinder-mold machine. This was invented to speed up the papermaking process. It has a deckle on two sides, created on the two outside (cylinder) edges.

In machine-made paper the paper pulp is run over the surface of steam-heated cylinders that dry it and set it up to be cut into sheets.

Paper Surfaces
The three main paper surfaces are hot-pressed, cold-pressed, and rough. Hot-pressed (abbreviated HP) is a smooth surface that is made by passing the paper through hot metal plates on rollers. Smooth, hard papers are generally used to print fine photographic halftones or detail. Cold-pressed (CP) paper is a surface between rough and smooth. This is made by running the sheets through cold metal rollers. Rough paper resembles watercolor paper and has the most grainy surface. This texture is the natural result of the papermaking process and is dried without re-pressing, so that the roughness is retained.

The toothy surface of cold-pressed and rough paper lends itself to printing textured images. When hand-drawn stencils that need to create a continuous tone are printed on a rough surface, particularly with a transparent ink, the texture of the paper increases the illusion. The color will appear to absorb in the depression of the paper and stand out in the peaks, giving a dark-and-light grainy effect. This can also occur with absorbent paper.

Acid is present in paper made of wood pulp and causes discoloration and deterioration. The paper used to print

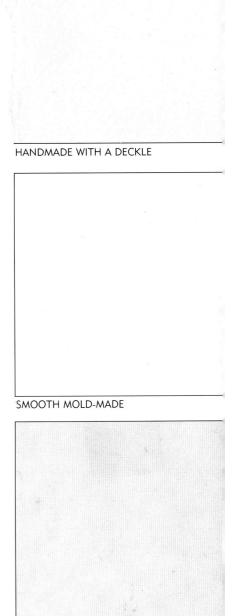

HANDMADE WITH A DECKLE

SMOOTH MOLD-MADE

RICE PAPER

Three different papers.

some of Hugh Kepets' prints was Arches Cover paper. This is a French mold-made paper that is 100-percent cotton rag and is acid-free. Fine-art editions need to be printed on acid-free paper. To be acid-free, paper has to have a neutral pH value. This is the balance between acid and alkaline components. Values of pH 6.5 to 7.5 are within the neutral range. Paper made from cotton rag, which is a replenishable resource, also does not require the destruction of trees.

Paper comes in various weights and sizes. Large sheets of paper should have a heavier weight, to give stability. Paper also comes sized or unsized. Sizing is a gelatin substance that is added in the papermaking process. Unsized paper (also called waterleaf) is very absorbent, which causes the ink to spread unnecessarily. The best paper for screenprinting is sized internally. This causes the paper to be stable and only absorb a small amount of ink.

I have printed on a variety of papers with excellent results. Oriental rice paper prints very well. My favorite is Arches Cover for its surface and stability. It also erases very easily. Lenox 100 is a good printing paper, as is Rives BFK. Other printers I know have good results with Coventry Rag and Stonehenge, to name just a few of the good quality papers available. You can also print water-based ink on coated or colored paper.

HANDLING PAPER

When you are screenprinting, the paper is moved hundreds of times. This can cause crimps in the paper if it is not handled correctly. A crimp is a dimpled impression in the paper, caused by the paper bending as it is picked up. Always grip it with both hands and keep it in a curve so that when you move it from the table to the rack, you do not damage it. This procedure should be followed every time the paper is moved.

FINAL PREPARATIONS

Once the stencil is on the screen, the color is mixed, and the paper is prepared, you are ready to print—almost.

Place your movable table next to the screen with your paper stacked on it.

Have a number of paper towels folded nearby with a full spray water bottle for easy access. Check the screen one last time for any pinholes that would allow ink to leak onto the paper in unwanted areas. Block out any that you find with screen filler or emulsion. Use a hair dryer to dry it quickly.

Checking Registration

Each sheet of paper must be placed under the screen in the exact same place every time you print—that is, it must have registration. Place the screen on the table with the flat side down and push the back of the screen into the hinge clamps. Tighten the clamps so the screen does not move from side to side. You should be looking into the screen so that the mesh is lying on the table. Always use one corner of the paper to register; I usually use the right-hand corner. Position the paper on the table so that it is centered under the open mesh of the stencil.

If the stencil on the screen was made with a separate positive (Rubylith, textured acetate, etc.), here is an easy way to register. Tape the positive onto the paper where you want to print it. Tape a piece of cardboard, or even a ruler, onto the paper. As you look through the screen, move the paper with the ruler or cardboard until the positive lines up with the open mesh of the stencil on the screen. Cut up three pieces of cardboard about 1" in length and width. Make sure the edge is sharp and straight. Tape the cardboard squares next to the paper; one on the right side two inches above the corner and two on the bottom on both ends of the sheet. Make sure they are taped securely so the paper will not slip underneath. Some printers use double-face tape or spray adhesive.

I wait until the color is printing correctly in the right spot before making my registration guides permanent; they may require adjustment. This form of registration ensures that the color will print in the exact same place on all the sheets of paper.

Checking the "Off-Contact"

The last thing to check before printing is the lift of the screen. Referred to as "off-contact," this simply means that the mesh of the screen should be resting slightly above the tabletop. When the ink is pulled across the screen with the squeegee, the mesh should snap off the print in an even, consistent way. This will ensure that the ink will print evenly through the stencil.

This even off-contact is particularly important with large, overall flat colors. When there is not enough space between the tabletop and the screen, the mesh slowly releases from the paper as the ink is printed. This leaves a strange rainbow mark in the printed color. If there is too much space and the off-contact is too high, the color will fail to print through every part of the stencil without enormous squeegee pressure.

Usually a tightly stretched screen and the lip of the hinge clamps will give the screen enough lift. If more is needed, evenly spaced rolled-up paper towels taped on the underside of the screen will do the trick. Use one towel on each side. Make sure the towels are far enough away from the stencil so that they do not interfere with the pull of the squeegee.

FLOODING THE SCREEN

In order to print a color, ink has to be pushed into the stencil before it is printed on the paper. This is called flooding the screen. Lift the screen up and hold it there with a block of wood. Pour a small amount of ink into the screen in front of the open part of the stencil. Hold the squeegee with a firm grip slightly slanted toward the screen and push ink across the surface so that it fills the open mesh. This flooding action should always be in the opposite direction from the print stroke that follows. You should see the color evenly saturate only the open mesh area. If the ink obliterates the shape of the stencil so that you cannot see it, you did not give it enough pressure.

If you have a vacuum, turn it on for the printing of the color. If the print does not cover all the holes of the vacuum chamber, cover the rest with newspaper or tape. This keeps the suction directly under the print. Remove the block and put the screen in the down position. While maintaining the angle of the squeegee, pull it across the screen with medium pressure. As the squeegee pulls across the stencil, the

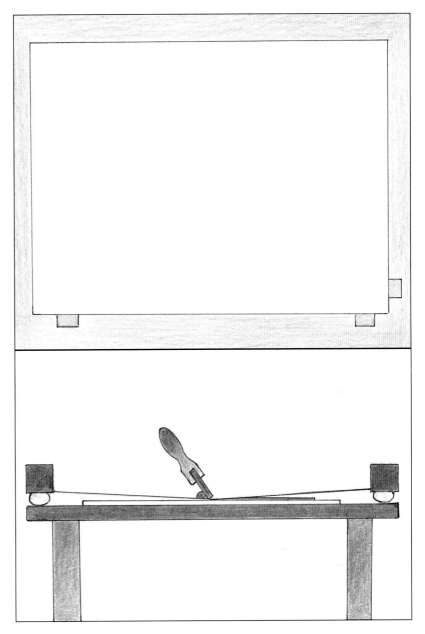

Top: The registration guides are placed next to the paper—two on the right-hand corner and one on the bottom left.

Bottom: As the squeegee moves over the screen, the mesh should snap up, releasing from the paper. This is called off-contact.

FLOODING THE SCREEN:

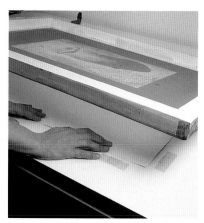

The paper is slid into the registration guides under the screen.

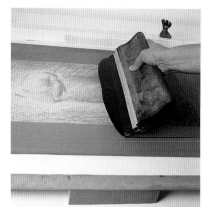

The squeegee is held on a slant and, here, pushed to the left to flood the screen. The screen is held up by a block of wood.

When printing, hold the squeegee firmly at a 45° angle and pull all the ink across the screen. Here, it is pulled to the right because the flooding of the screen was done with a leftward pull.

After the rabbit drawing is printed, it is checked for printing flaws.

The completed rabbit print.

screen should release from the paper where the color has already been printed, because of the off-contact. If this did not occur, it could be due to several things:

1. The lift is not high enough.
2. The ink is too thick.
3. The screen is not stretched tightly.

Once you print the color, lift up the screen and put the block of wood in place to hold it. Flood the screen before you remove the paper. (Again, flood it in the opposite direction from the print stroke.) This helps to keep the ink from drying in the screen while you check the print. If the color looks fine, place the sheet on the drying rack and continue printing.

PRINTING WITH A ONE-ARM SQUEEGEE

The one-arm squeegee is balanced with weights to help make printing large-scale prints easier. The amount of pressure that the printer applies to the arm is distributed evenly and requires less effort than a hand squeegee to achieve the same result. The squeegee's pressure can be adjusted, and the slant of the squeegee can be changed by the screws on the metal base.

The screen is secured at the back of the table with an alan key, and a clamp is attached on each side of the screen in the front. The side front clamps are hooked to the back of the one-arm assembly with chains. Hold the screen in the up position when you attach the chains. The screen should remain in this position when you let go of it. It should also be easy to put it in the down position. If it is not, adjust the weights at the back of the table. The screen should also look balanced when it is in the up position. One side should not be lower than the other. The height of the screen in the up position should be comfortable for registering the paper and removing a print. If it is too low, you cannot see under the screen; if it is too high, the ink will constantly flow to the back of the table.

With very large prints, I make a platform in front of the printing table to stand on. This allows me (because I am short) to lean over the squeegee as I push it across. The screen is held in an

1

2

USING A ONE-ARM SQUEEGEE:

1. The edition of David Grubb's *Hybrid Pink* is printed with a one-arm squeegee. The print is placed under the screen into the registration guides.

2. Pouring the ink into the screen.

3. While the screen is held up with one hand, the squeegee is pulled across the screen with the other hand to flood it.

4. Pushing the ink across the screen and printing the colors.

5. Removing the print from the table after the color is printed.

6. The prints are placed in the drying rack.

3

4

5

6

PROGRESSIVE PROOFS:

This is a set of progressive proofs of Grubb's *Hybrid Pink*. A set of progressive proofs is kept to record the progress. They serve as a reference point when printing fine-art editions. When there are multiple layers of transparent colors being printed, an accurate record of each color in the progression is necessary. It would be difficult to tell what color went before or after without this record.

For *Hybrid Pink*, the first progressive proof, Proof #1, was the overall drawing printed in a mauve color.

The second proof, Proof #2, that I set aside had color #1, the drawing, and three additional colors—blue and two different pinks on the flowers.

Proof #3 has an additional three colors added to the flower on the left.

Proof # 1

Proof # 2

Proof # 3

Proof #4 also has three added colors, but a much more dramatic change occurs because of the overall yellow-green. A light blue and dark pink are also printed. The yellow-green is transparent enough for the texture of the drawing (color #1) to be clearly seen. This gives the print an added color.

Four more colors in Proof #5 change the look of the print further: another overall green, a black texture, a third blue, and a transparent yellow orange on the flower on the left. This flower color also prints on the pink petal to create yet another color.

Proof # 4

Proof #6 is the last one pulled before the final print. It contains a darker green texture on the lily pads, a transparent black that prints over the green texture so that it shows through, and a transparent whitish blue on the petals and in accents on the lily pads.

Proof # 5

Proof # 6

Four more colors were printed to complete the image: a brown, a very light blue in the background, an ochre, and a touch of yellow-green to accent the pods and the bud. A total of twenty-one colors were printed to complete the proof. Once the proof is finished and approved by the artist, the edition is printed.

David Grubb, *Hybrid Pink*, 31¹/₂ x 47¹/₂" (80 x 120.5 cm). The finished print is an edition of sixty, plus artist's proofs. Printed by the author and published by Orion Editions.

upright position with one hand, and the squeegee arm is pulled across the screen toward you with the other hand to flood it. Put the screen down, making sure that all the ink that you flooded is in front of the squeegee ready to print.

If the table has a vacuum, turn it on during the printing stroke and off when the screen is flooded.

Place one hand on the handle and the other farther up on the arm. Push the ink away from you and across the screen as you print. Always look to see that the screen is printing off-contact— that is, the mesh is releasing from the paper as the color prints. Immediately lift up the screen and flood it again to prevent the ink from drying. Check the quality of the printed color. Look for streaks, dried-in areas, rainbow marks, and so on. This is when you will see if the stencil is correct to the image. If it looks good, continue printing. If not, try to identify the problem and correct it. Always use proof paper until the screen is printing correctly.

PRINTING TIPS

Always approach printing in a precise, methodical way to avoid problems. Pay attention to all the small details. Have all your supplies—filled water bottles, paper towels, tape—in a convenient location. This will help if it becomes necessary to stop in the middle of printing to correct something. For example, if ink has leaked through the stencil in the wrong place and you need a piece of tape to stop it, searching for the tape could allow the ink to dry in the screen and present another problem.

Keep everything clean. Avoid dripping ink on the side of the can. This can easily get on the table and on your hands. Many a print has been ruined with ink fingerprints.

Water-based ink builds up on the inside of the screen as you print, unlike oil-based ink, which has a slippery quality as it moves across the surface. It is advisable to scoop the ink out and return it to the container to thin it when this happens. Add a little water or a retarder and mix it thoroughly before returning it to the screen. This will minimize the buildup and keep the ink's viscosity—its ability to flow—consistent. I also spray water very lightly on the sides of the stencil as I print to minimize the buildup. Make sure the water does not get into the open stencil, for this will change the color that is printing.

When there is more than one stencil on a screen, they must be printed one at a time. Block out one of the stencils with wide cellophane tape on the squeegee side of the screen, for blocking from the underside of the screen would allow the ink from the first printing to dry in the second stencil. Also, an emulsion stencil remains cold during printing and is resistant to tape from underneath. I also tape the paper towels with very sticky cellophane tape for this reason.

Make sure that the mesh remains open when you print textures or fine details, as in halftones. Always look at the screen when the squeegee moves across the image. You will be able to see if the ink is drying in the screen. It appears as distinctly darker edges of the colors that are trapped in the mesh, preventing the fluid ink from printing there. The image will start to lose the details, and it will look as if less and less is printing on the paper. Make sure there is enough retarder in the ink to slow the drying process when this happens. Spray water on a paper towel and wash the edges that have dried before flooding. Print on some proof paper until the details are correct again.

If too much detail is printing, wipe the underside of the screen with a dry paper towel before flooding and then continue the printing sequence. I have also flooded the screen and printed without pulling all the ink across, so that only the ink in the mesh is printed. This gives a lighter, cleaner print of detail in a textured stencil. The flood then has to be pushed in the opposite direction. For example, you flood the screen to the left. You leave the ink, but print the screen. Now flood to the right with the leftover ink, but always print in the same direction, or the registration changes because of the stretching of the screen.

The squeegee angle (45°) and sharpness are very important. The blade must also be very straight, with no hills and valleys. If the registration guides are too large or close to the printing area, they will interfere with the squeegee and the ink will not print in those spots. Make sure the guides are not much thicker than the printing paper when this happens. Always print into the registration guides. If your guides are in the right-hand corner, print into that corner. When there is excess movement as you print, put a C clamp at the end of the frame of the screen. This should also be the same corner that you print into.

PRINTING PROBLEMS

The following are some common problems that develop during the screen-printing process, along with some recommended solutions.

Stencil Breakdown: If ink is coming through in unwanted areas, the cause may be pinholes in the stencil that were not blocked out. If it is just a dot or two, you can cover the holes with very sticky cellophane tape on the underside of the screen. Masking tape will not stick, for the emulsion is made cold and resistant by the water-based ink. If it is a major breakdown and the stencil appears weak, it was not hardened enough in front of an ultraviolet light. You must remake the screen and harden it longer.

Dried-in Ink on Stencil Edges: This is caused by taking too long between printings or not enough retarder in the ink. Remove the ink from the screen and add retarder. Wash the screen with water to open up the dried-in edges. Make sure you dry the screen with a hair dryer before resuming printing.

Squashed-out Ink on the Edges: When the ink prints under the stencil and blurs on the edges, the squeegee stroke is usually to blame. If you flip the squeegee up at the end of the stroke, it can push the ink under the stencil. Keep the angle of the squeegee at 45° and constant from one end of the screen to the other. This should correct the problem, but the ink could also be too thin. Remix it. There are binders that you can add to thicken the ink.

Uneven Color: When the color is not consistent, it could be caused by squeegee pressure. Make sure the

squeegee is pressing down equally on all parts of the stencil.

Streaks in the Color: When streaks of other colors appear in the printing color, it is the result of poor mixing. Remove the color and mix it thoroughly. If the dots of color persist, it is necessary to strain the ink. Force the ink through a finer mesh with a spatula into a clean container. This will remove the hardened dots of color. When streaks are not caused by color, it is usually the squeegee. Remove it from the screen and wash off the ink. Feel the edge to see if it is rough. If so, rub fine steel wool over the edge to make it smooth.

Squashed Halftone or Texture: When a photographic halftone is not printing cleanly with all of the detail, but is filling in, you may need to use one of the available halftone bases that keep the ink from squashing. Also, check several things:

1. Make sure it is printing off-contact.

2. The flood stroke may be too heavy. Try printing without bringing all the ink across.

3. Wipe the screen gently after each printing with a dry paper towel on the underside of the screen.

4. The paper that you are printing on may be too rough. Halftones print best on smooth paper.

Ink Stays Tacky: Too much retarder was added. Only 10 percent of the ink should be retarder.

Poor Registration: When the registration is not holding and the colors are not aligning with each other, check all of the following:

1. Is the screen moving? Tighten the clamps to hold it securely.

2. Check the registration guides. Make sure each sheet of paper exactly abuts the guides, and do not let the paper slip under or over them. It is hard to tell when the first color prints if it is in the right place. There are no other colors to check it against. It is when the second color is printed that the registration problems show. If each sheet has a different registration, it is hard to correct. If the color is still out of register on the first few prints, change the registration

guides to move the prints into the correct register.

Rainbow Marks in the Printed Color: Whenever a strange pattern, usually occurring in a half-circle, appears, it is called a rainbow. This is caused when the mesh does not release from the printed ink fast enough during printing. Usually there is not enough lift, and the screen needs to print more off-contact. The screen may also be stretched too loosely. Use paper towels rolled up under the screen to help it snap off the print. Or thin the ink a little. It may be too thick.

Above:
Andrea Callard, *Fly Paper*,
30 x 22" (76.2 x 56 cm).
This six-color print was done on Mulberry rice paper from Japan. Published by Avocet.

Opposite page:
Gretchen Dow Simpson, *Jamestown*,
27³/₄ x 22³/₄" (70.5 x 57.8 cm).
Printed on Coventry rag paper, this work was printed at Noblet Serigraphic, Inc., New York, and published by Pamplemousse Press.

Mark Williams, *World 1987*,
31¹/₂ x 47¹/₄" (80 x 120 cm).
A large work printed by the
author at the Screenprint
Workshop on Arches Cover
paper.

PROOFING A PRINT

The proofing process is a way to test the stencils, screens, and inks before printing an entire edition. Usually fifteen to twenty-five sheets of paper are printed. This allows the printer and artist to see if the color separations are correct.

The print *Hybrid Pink* by David Grubb was proofed with a one-arm squeegee at the Screenprint Workshop (see pp. 97-100). The original art is an acrylic painting on paper. The print was made smaller than the original by having a photographically reduced print made at a color lab. This was used as a guide to make the stencils.

Grubb, an artist who wanted as much involvement in the printing process as possible, made a master drawing on acetate with black china markers. This became the first stencil, printed as a transparent mauve. It was used as a "key plate" for all the colors to register to. The stencils for the flowers were printed next, so that the color relationships between the shades of blue of the water stencil could be seen better. To print the correct blues without the bright flowers for comparison would be difficult. Several stencils were made, and the colors were printed before the next stencils were made. David worked on most of the stencils to maintain the character of his hand in the print.

INSPECTING THE PRINTS

After the edition is completed, the prints are checked for flaws. These can be in the form of fingerprints, spots of ink in the borders, or misregistration. Fingerprints are often easily removed with a kneaded eraser. Most spots of ink can be gently scraped off with a razor blade if you use the blade to shave the spots; don't try to dig them out with the point of the razor.

Most printers keep small amounts of the printed colors to touch up spots on the prints where the ink misprinted. This must be done very carefully so it is not detectable. Edges can be restored using a razor blade on an angle, and pressed only lightly into the paper. Using a brush, you paint the color on the print and blade. When the razor is lifted, the edge will be straight. When the ink has printed over the edge, use a ruler and lightly score the ink where it is protruding. Take the razor and, with the ruler still in place, gently shave the ink away. The scored line will keep the edge sharp. These flaws must be minor, and even then these measures will work well only on good 100-percent cotton rag paper.

SIGNING THE EDITION

Adding to the value of the print is the limit on the number of copies that are made. Printing fewer copies increases the value. The number of prints in an edition is decided before the prints are made. The extra prints are destroyed (or used for proof paper), and the stencils and screens are reclaimed. The David Grubb print, *Hybrid Pink* was an edition of sixty prints with ten artist's proofs and two printer's proofs.

The print edition is always signed and numbered in pencil. Traditionally, the signature is in the right-hand corner, but this is not mandatory. The edition number is commonly in the left-hand corner. In the past, the edition number always indicated printing order. In the case of etchings, the lower numbers are still favored, for the quality of the print diminishes toward the end of the edition. But in screenprinting the first print and the last are equal in quality, so the numbering of the prints is just a kind of listing of each print. For example, the numbering sequence for the Grubb edition was as follows: 1/60 designates the first print out of the total number of prints in the edition; 2/60 designates the second print, and so on to the last print, numbered 60/60. The artist's and printer's proofs are numbered separately.

THE CHOP MARK

Finally, the printer's identifying mark, called a chop mark, is put on each print at the end of the signing, usually in the left-hand corner below the edition number. This is the logo of the shop that made the edition, and it is embossed into the paper.

OIL-BASED VS. WATER-BASED PRINTING

The first and immediate contrast is the lack of solvent fumes evaporating into your face as you print with water-based inks, and the elimination of noisy exhaust systems, which never did remove all the fumes. These, of course, are the contrasts to the actual printing environment.

The differences in printing quality are none, but there are differences in the way the ink feels and moves. Water-based ink must not be allowed to dry in the screen, because it is more difficult to remove it without destroying the stencil. It is not equally difficult with all the brands of ink, however. There are retarders to prevent this. Again, these act as a flow agent to keep the mesh open during normal printing. When a problem like stencil breakdown arises, you must remove the ink from the screen and clean it thoroughly with water before you can fix the problem. With oil-based ink, if it dries in the screen it can always be removed with solvents without damage to the stencil. If it is just a matter of dots of ink breaking through the stencil, a piece of tape can be placed over the area where the ink is coming through, on the underside of the screen. To prevent this with oil-based ink, masking tape is usually used. With water-based ink, the emulsion stencil is resistant to masking tape; it doesn't stick to the emulsion very long. Wide cellophane tape, which is very sticky, works the best in this case.

The consistency of water-based ink is slightly looser than that of the oil-based. As noted before, it builds up on the screen during printing and must be scooped out periodically and returned to the can to be thinned down to maintain a smooth flow.

The quality of the water-based ink in terms of color and surface is excellent, and the ease with which it can be cleaned with just a spray water bottle makes the other inconveniences well worth the switch.

Chapter 7

Different Applications

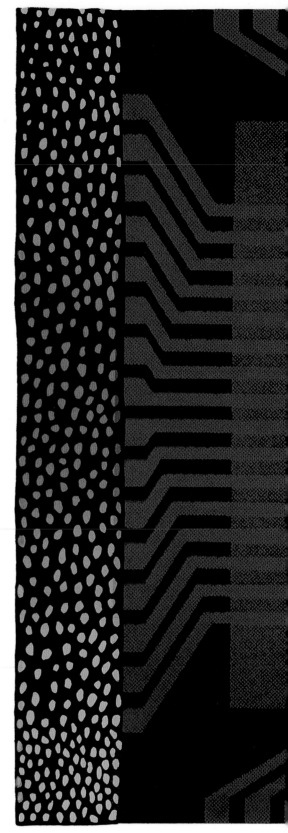

O il-based screenprinting has always been used for printing on different surfaces by the commercial industries. These include surfaces as varied as plastic bottles, telephone circuits, and children's wooden toys. Many advertising billboards have been screenprinted. Of course, different results occur according to the quality of the surface (rough, smooth, hard, or porous), and the oil-based inks are formulated to accommodate each one of these surfaces. Water-based ink is equally as versatile, with some limitations. For example, there is no comparable water-based enamel ink, and some of the inks formulated for printing on plastics have high degrees of toxicity, even though they are water-based.

Carter Hodgekin,
Transmission Dreaming,
15 3/8 x 22 1/2" (39 x 57 cm).
This computer chip image, printed with
bronze powder in Createx base, has a color
blend on either side. It was made by the artist
and Andrea Collard and published by Avocet.

FABRIC

There are specific water-based inks designed to print on fabric; the textile industry has used them for years. These inks have less ground pigment and more base than the inks formulated for use on paper. The consistency, which is similar to mayonnaise, allows the ink to penetrate the fabric. It actually soaks into the material. Once the ink is printed, it must be heat-treated to make it permanent. This is called *curing*. Professional textile printers have a system of curing the ink that allows the fabric to pass through a dryer. Artists who simply want to print a tee shirt or a piece of fabric with their image can use an iron to cure the ink. It is best to iron on the inside of the fabric or shirt, and not on the ink side, using a medium heat setting.

Even though water-based textile ink has been around for many years, it could not be utilized to print well on paper. This is because of the lower ratio of pigment to base (the vehicle that the pigment is suspended or dissolved in). Less pigment produces less intensity of color on paper, and more base creates buckling and misregistration when printed on paper. On occasion I find a textile ink that is usable on paper, but it is the exception rather than the rule.

Printing Tee Shirts

The same set-up procedure as outlined in Chapter 6, on printing, is used to print this group of children's tee shirts. The screen for the zebra image is placed on a simple printing table with hinge clamps and secured.

MATERIALS

PREPARED SCREEN
TEE SHIRTS
WATER-BASED TEXTILE INK
PLASTIC CONTAINERS FOR MIXING INK
SPATULAS
SCOOP CARDS (CUT PIECES OF ILLUSTRATION BOARD OR FOAMCORE)
TAPE (MASKING AND CELLOPHANE)
PAPER TOWELS
CARDBOARD CUT TO FIT INSIDE THE TEE SHIRT
ADHESIVE SPRAY
SPRAY WATER BOTTLE

The registration of the shirt calls for a slight alteration. Because it is made of a porous cotton fabric that stretches, the shirt is mounted on a piece of cardboard that is cut to fit snugly inside the shirt.

These tee shirts were screenprinted and hand-colored. The zebra was printed twice with black Deka-Print textile ink to achieve a rich solid color. The dog and dog doll had three different printings: the doll was printed first and sewn and stuffed later. The orange, black, and yellow of the fish were printed, but the green was hand-colored.

Equal-sized pieces of cardboard are cut for each shirt and, before being put inside the shirts, are sprayed with adhesive. The shirt is flattened down on the adhesive which keeps it from moving during the printing process.

Of course, the wrinkles must be smoothed out. The sleeves and bottom of the shirt are pulled and folded behind the cardboard and taped with masking tape. This makes the front of the shirt, where it will be printed, very smooth. It also sets up the edges of the cardboard to fit into the registration guides. Because the shirt is bulky on the cardboard and not flat like a sheet of paper, the guides must be made of thicker cardboard so that the shirt does not slip over the guides. Either build up several pieces of illustration board to use as guides or use cut-up foamcore. I use four guides, instead of three (as with paper)—two at the bottom and one on each side.

The screen is flooded and printed in the same way as with paper, except when the color is not covering with a good intensity. Then it can be printed and flooded again. The black ink of the zebra tee shirt was printed and reflooded with the screen in the down position twice to get the black rich and even.

Remember first to proof the screen on paper (newspaper or the back of old prints will do) before printing a shirt. This makes sure the screen is printing correctly. Once that is determined, if the shirt doesn't print well, you will know it is not the screen. Look for another explanation, such as:

1. Not enough squeegee pressure. This will cause a very weak printing. The color is not saturated enough and areas of the image are not even.

2. Too much squeegee pressure. This makes the ink print out of the stencil area, so it looks as if the color is squashing onto the shirt.

3. The angle of the squeegee is too straight. Not enough ink is printing through the stencil.

4. The angle of the squeegee is too slanted. The ink is pushing under the stencil and squashing out of the image area.

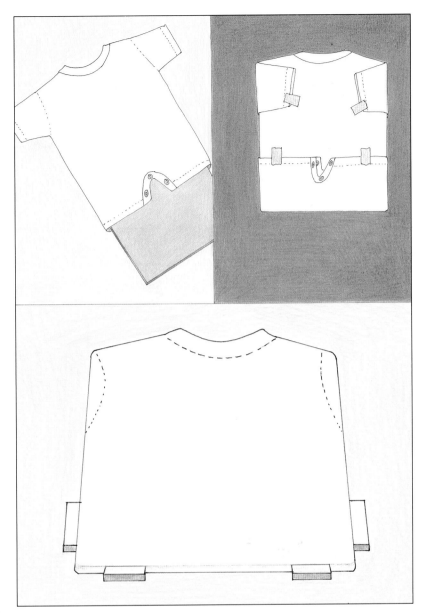

5. Improper flooding of the screen. You should review the procedure described on pp. 95-96.

Professional tee shirt printers have a system of printing multiple colors on shirts that may employ four screens and an area that the shirt fits into. When one screen is finished printing, a second moves into its place while the shirt remains in register. This speeds up the process considerably and keeps the cost of printing multicolored tee shirts quite low.

Artists use fabrics to print on, even canvas, to add another dimension to their art. There is no fitting, taping, and buildup of guides necessary. Again, the fabric can be held in place with spray adhesive. Spray it onto a printing table

Top, left: The cardboard is precut to fit inside the tee shirt.

Top, right: The sleeves and bottom of the shirt are folded back and secured with masking tape.

Bottom: The registration tabs must be made high enough to prevent the shirt from moving. These were made from foamcore.

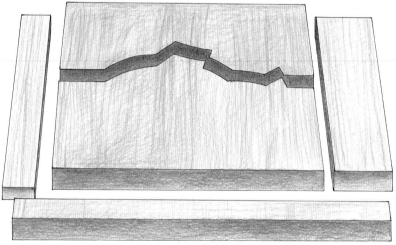

Top: This coat rack was screened with five colors. The water-based ink was T.W. Graphics' 1000 line.

Bottom: The wood from which the coat rack was cut is placed around the rack to form a jig. This makes a smooth surface for the squeegee to pass over.

and place the material over it in register to the image on the screen. Flatten it down to keep it from moving. If the material is very porous, it may need more than one printing. Canvas can be printed raw (and very absorbent), or it can be painted with gesso or paint to make it less porous.

WOOD, PLASTIC, AND GLASS

Wood presents a surface that is less porous than that of fabric. The ink sits on the wood and is not absorbed very easily. Conventional water-based ink prints very well on this surface. Artists can incorporate the wood grain into their imagery or eliminate it by sanding the wood and priming it with gesso or paint. The surface can be made very smooth.

Since the screen must print off-contact, it is necessary to raise it to accommodate the thickness of the wood. This is done when the screen is placed in the hinge clamps. Raise it as high as the thickness of the wood by putting wood pieces under the frame when it is secured in the clamps. Obviously there is a limit as to the height the screen can be raised. Depending on what is to be printed, a jig must be made to form around the wood.

For example, the wood for the children's coat rack (see illustration) was precut before printing. The pieces of wood that it was cut from were kept to make a jig that fits around the rack. This enables the screen to lie on one flat surface. This way, the squeegee will pass smoothly over the wood. Otherwise, with only the coat rack resting under the screen, the squeegee would not print an even layer of ink. Instead, it would force the ink to fail to print on the edge of the wood or to blob over it.

This particular image was printed in five colors. The sides and top were not screened, but painted. The holes for the dowels were drilled after the printing, and the dowels were hand-painted to match the purple background.

This was a commercial venture, but artists have printed on wood and used the images as a base for three-dimensional projects. In those cases, the wood has been printed and cut after.

Plastic and glass are smooth, so the ink will not be absorbed but will sit on the surface. Choose the brand of ink that gives you the most opacity. The only special consideration when printing on plastic or glass is its thickness. Make sure your set-up, as in printing wood, accommodates the thickness.

COLOR BLENDING

One way to print continuous tone, in addition to the methods already covered in Chapter 3, does not require a photographic or hand-drawn stencil: blending the colors directly on the screen. This method produces varied results, as the blended area changes every time a print is made.

To print a color blend, use a stencil method that creates an open mesh. This could be Rubylith film, painted acetates, or even emulsion-blocked screen. The screen mesh should also be chosen according to how heavy a deposit of ink you want. Color blends can be printed with opaque or transparent inks. For a heavier deposit of ink use a coarser mesh of 180–200, and for a thinner deposit a mesh of 230–260. Once the screen is made, place it on the printing table and follow the same procedure that is covered in Chapter 5, on printing. Since it is an open mesh, make sure it will print off-contact.

You can do a blend only along a borderline between colors that follows the direction that the squeegee is pulled. As should become clear, if you are printing from side to side with a hand or one-arm squeegee, the blend will go from top to bottom across the borderline; whereas pulling a hand squeegee toward you from top to bottom will give you a blend from side to side.

It is possible to print the blend on an angle if the squeegee moves on an angle. The blend will follow the movement of the squeegee.

Make sure you have extra proof paper to print on. Use old sheets of paper or newspaper to get the blend printing smoothly. Pour the colors that you want to blend on the screen on either side—for example, blue and pink. Blue is poured halfway up the screen, and pink is poured on the other half. The borderline where they meet is at the midway point. Take a scoop card and push the two colors back and forth until they start to blend into each other. Be careful not to get the ink in the open mesh. When the colors start to mix, replace the scoop card with a squeegee and continue to move the ink back and forth until it blends further.

Now put a sheet of proof paper in place and flood the screen. You will be able to see if the color is blending smoothly by looking under the screen at the flooded area. Print it and reflood it. You will have to print proofs until the blend prints evenly. Then print on your edition paper.

Try to keep the blend as consistent as possible. When it begins to change too much from your original blend, remove the ink. Start over with fresh ink and repeat the process. The two colors that are blending change in a variety of ways. Sometimes one color overpowers the other. What starts out as blue on one side and pink on the other becomes all blue or all pink with just a touch of the other color. This will occur more quickly if the consistency of the two colors is different. It is very important to keep one from being more viscous than the other. (Viscosity, the ability to flow, depends upon the ink's thickness).

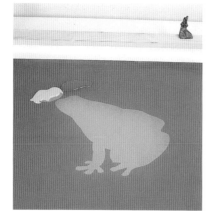

The two colors are placed next to each other.

A scoop card is used to push the two colors back and forth to start the colors blending.

The squeegee replaces the scoop card and continues blending the color.

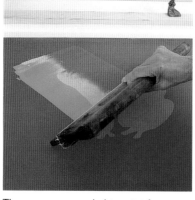

The squeegee, angled to print from the top of the frog's back to its feet, is pulled across the image. An angled squeegee will make a blend along a diagonal.

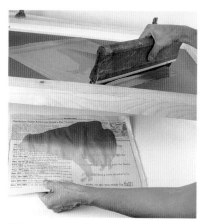

After many printings on proof paper, the blend is getting smoother.

The color blend is printing correctly.

Another factor is the slant of the screen when it is flooded. Try to keep it lower than normal, for the ink moves back and forth as the screen moves up and down between flooding and printing. Some printing tables are raised in the back, and this also makes the ink flow.

Printing a color blend requires patience. Once the blend is printing smoothly, expect to get eight to ten good printings before the ink needs to be changed. Every time new ink is added, it will take the same number of printings as in the beginning to blend evenly again.

In the following example, a frog print is made with two color blends.

MATERIALS

THREE PREPARED SCREENS
(ONE FOR EACH BLEND)
INK AND CONTAINERS
SQUEEGEE
SCOOP CARDS
SPATULA
TAPE (MASKING AND CELLOPHANE)
SPRAY WATER BOTTLE
PAPER TOWELS
PAPER

The frog print is made with three Rubylith stencils—one for the background and two for the frog. One frog stencil has a color blend that is angled from the top left corner to the bottom right corner. The first color printed is the overall shape of the frog in a blend of orange and yellow: orange on the top of the frog and yellow on the bottom. The Rubylith stencil is overcut, slightly larger than the frog, to allow for trapping. The second blend is the background. This stencil is cut to the correct size to fit around the frog. It is printed from side to side so that the colors, dark aqua (on the top) and light aqua (on the bottom), will blend along a horizontal line. That is, there is one area of blending: the boundary where the dark aqua on the top meets the light aqua on the bottom. The last color printed is the black pattern of the frog.

Cleaning Up

The cleanup after printing a color blend follows the same procedure outlined in Chapter 8. The only difference is the

disposal of the ink in the screen after printing. Usually the colors have blended together so much that they cannot be returned to the original containers. After doing the frog print, I scooped all the colors from each screen into three community containers, the blue mixture in one, the yellow-orange in another, and the black into a third. These colors can be used to mix with fresh color when matching colors for future prints. The stencils are removed from the screens as outlined in the section on stencil removal in Chapter 8.

WAX CRAYONS

Different textures can be made by drawing onto the screen with wax crayons. Any brand will work. The crayons act as a resist to the ink, so that what prints is the opposite of what you draw. The best results are obtained by introducing distinctive textures such as those of window screens or wire mesh, or by printing on rough watercolor paper. This method can be combined with painting emulsion directly onto the screen. Oil pastels can also be used as a resist when drawn on the screen.

MATERIALS

STRETCHED SCREEN (200–230 MESH)
CRAYONS
TEXTURED SURFACES (WIRE MESH, ETC.)
EMULSION
INK
SCOOP CARDS
SPATULA
PAPER TOWELS
SPRAY WATER BOTTLE
TAPE

Making a Textured Wax Crayon Screen

Begin with a textured surface that you want to reproduce. For this illustration, I chose a stiff wire window screen,

The finished print is a combination of two color blends: one angled and one vertical. The last color is the black pattern.

A piece of wire window screen is used to make a "drawn-on" texture.

The wire is placed under the screen, and the image is drawn with a wax crayon.

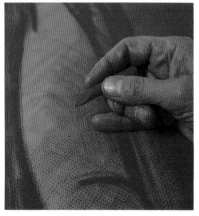

This closeup shows the texture that is achieved with the window screen. It almost looks like a coarse halftone.

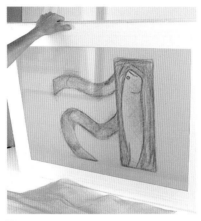

The screen is held up to a light to see if there is enough of a crayon buildup.

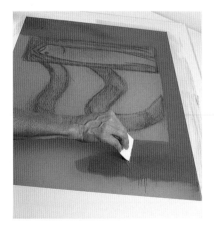

After the drawing is completed, the screen is blocked out with emulsion, except where it should print.

The image has been printed on wood, and the artist is hand-coloring the fish.

which I put under the mesh of the screen flat side down. Using a drawing of a fish as a reference, I drew with a maroon crayon on the inside of the screen over the wire texture.

The screen should have good contact with the texture. If it does not, build it up from underneath with cardboard. The crayon fills in the mesh of the screen. Always build up more crayon on the screen than you would on paper. Once the drawing was finished, I heated it with a hair dryer to make the crayon last longer. I then filled in the borders with emulsion.

The image will print the opposite of the drawing. In order to capture the look of the maroon crayon drawing, I printed the drawing with a light color on a piece of maroon-tinted wood. The rest of the print was hand-colored.

This method is also good for repairing textured stencils that have been shot onto the screen with acetate and emulsion. If a section of a textured stencil has to be removed because it is incorrect or has opened up, you can draw it back in using wax crayons.

Cleaning Up

The cleanup of the ink is the same here as with all the other printing methods. However, the crayon must be removed with a spray-on household cleanser. Any brand that specifies its wax-removing ability will do. Just spray the cleanser on and let it sit for thirty minutes, then wipe it off with sponges or paper towels. Stubborn spots can be cleaned with scrub brushes and powdered cleanser, such as Ajax or Comet. The emulsion stencil must be removed with bleach (see Chapter 8). Oil pastels can be removed with laundry prewash products, such as Shout or Spray 'n' Wash.

PAINTING POSITIVE IMAGES

Liquid drawing fluid is available to paint a positive image directly on the screen without the use of acetate. This can simulate the artist's painted stroke. What you paint on the screen will eventually become the open mesh of the screen, making the method similar to painting on acetate (see Chapter 3). The difference is in quality and directness. I use this method for more spontaneous

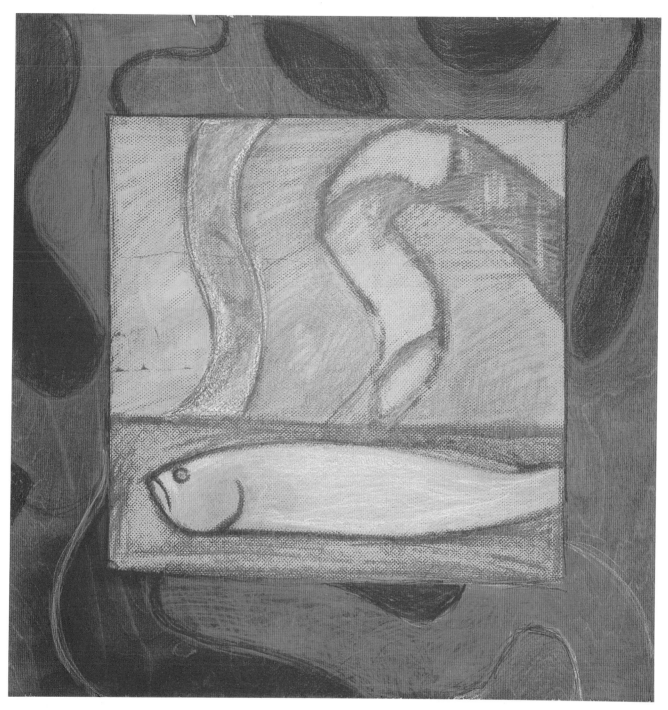

The finished print, made by the wax crayon method, printed on wood, and hand-colored.

PAINTING POSITIVE IMAGES:

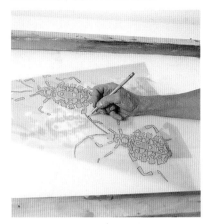

The screen is placed over the water-color and the black shape of the insect is drawn by the artist.

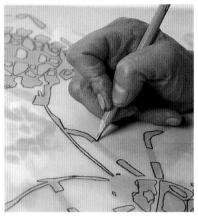

This closeup shows the black lines clearly.

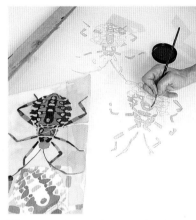

The screen is turned over and, using the watercolor as a reference, the black insect shapes are painted with drawing fluid.

The screen filler is coated over the painted stencil image. A thin coat will prevent the filler from penetrating the drawing and making it impossible to wash out.

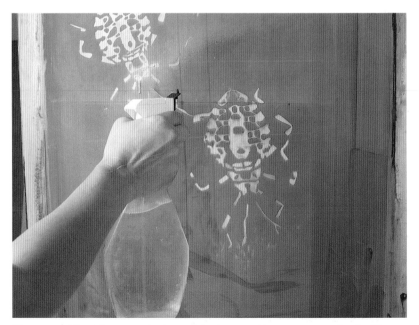

The screen filler is being washed out of the screen with a spray water bottle. The originally painted area then becomes the open mesh of the screen.

and experimental printing. It is very direct and does not need to be applied to the screen by exposure to ultraviolet light. What it lacks for fine-art edition printing is consistency and a separate stencil for reference.

MATERIALS

SCREEN (230 WHITE MONOFILAMENT)
HUNT'S LIQUID DRAWING FLUID
HUNT'S SCREEN FILLER
BRUSHES FOR PAINTING
HAIR DRYER OR FAN
SCOOP COATER OR SCOOP CARDS
WATER-BASED INK
SQUEEGEE
MASKING AND CELLOPHANE TAPE
PAPER TOWELS
SPATULA
SPRAY WATER BOTTLE
BLEACH
CLEANSER AND SCRUB BRUSH
GLOVES

Using a brush and some drawing fluid, paint the image directly onto the screen. Either follow a pencil drawing on the screen or simply "ad lib" and develop an image from an idea. Once the drawing is completed, dry it thoroughly with a hair dryer or fan. If you draw on the inside of the screen, the image will print correctly; but if you draw on the outside, the image will be reversed when it prints.

Coat the screen on the same side as the drawing with screen filler. Use a squeegee or a scoop coater and apply it the same way you would photo emulsion (see Chapter 4), in one thin coat. Make sure that you paint a thick coat of drawing fluid, because if the screen filler penetrates the drawing fluid, it will not wash out.

If edges tend to become ragged during washing, they can be touched up with screen filler and a brush.

Dry the screen thoroughly, and then place the screen in a washout stand and spray it with warm water. The positive drawing will wash out, and the screen filler will remain. Thus, the open mesh will be the positive drawing. Dry the screen again and check for pinholes in the filler. If there are some, touch them up with more filler. Print the screen following the same procedure as in Chapter 5, on printing. The bug pattern

The finished image of the insects is printed on hand-painted homosote board and assembled into a planter.

on the planter above was made with screens painted with drawing fluid.

Almost any water-soluble fluid can be used to paint on the screen as long as it will resist the screen filler. Make sure it has a good consistency for painting. I've used Karo syrup colored with ink. Once you understand the principle, you can experiment to create interesting patterns on a screen by spraying or spattering the drawing fluid with almost anything—a stiff toothbrush, a sponge, and so on.

Cleaning Up

The screen filler can be removed from the screen with bleach or a strong cleanser like Top Job. Soak the screen with the bleach and lay paper towels or newspapers on top. Keep the towels and newspapers wet with the bleach. Let it stand for thirty to forty minutes until the filler loosens. Wash it off with hot water in a washout stand. It can also be removed with spray water bottles to conserve water. Remove stubborn stains and spots with a stiff nylon brush and cleanser such as Ajax or Comet.

MONOPRINTS

Traditionally, a monoprint, as the name implies, is a one-time image that is created with a printing process; monoprints are commonly made with an etching or lithographic press. The artist draws or paints an image on a sheet of acrylic, such as Plexiglas, or on an etching plate using oil paints or etching inks. A piece of paper is placed over the drawing and is cranked through the press. The printed image, a reverse of the drawing, is unique and cannot be duplicated.

Screened monoprints are drawn or painted directly onto the mesh of the screen, but they are not strictly limited to a one-time printing. Once your image is completed on the screen, transparent base is used as a vehicle to transfer it onto the paper. I frequently can get two or three more light images to transfer in this way.

The character of this printed image is unlike a drawing or painting, of course, for the printing process adds its own dimension that is often intriguing.

You can use a wide variety of water-soluble materials to make an image. I've had good results with water-soluble crayons and pencils and also watercolor and gouache. Different materials afford different results. Unlike etching monoprints, which are made only on paper, screenprinted monoprints can be printed on surfaces other than paper, such as wood or fabric.

SCREEN (200–230 WHITE MONOFILAMENT)
SQUEEGEE
PHOTO EMULSION
SCOOP CARD OR BRUSH
HALIDE OR ULTRAVIOLET LAMP
WATER-SOLUBLE CRAYONS AND PENCILS
WATERCOLOR AND GOUACHE
PAPER TOWELS
SPRAY WATER BOTTLE
TRANSPARENT BASE
   (ANY WATER-SOLUBLE BRAND)
GLOVES

Begin the monoprint by preparing the screen with photo emulsion. First, choose a size and shape and draw it directly onto the screen with a pencil. Usually this is a square or a rectangle. Block it out with emulsion so that the mesh remains open within the drawn shape. It can be blocked out with a scoop card or a brush, or both. Next, dry the screen thoroughly and harden it in front of a halide lamp or comparable ultraviolet light for five minutes (or in even daylight for twenty-five minutes).

Set the screen up on the printing table or raise it off the ground with blocks. Draw on the inside of the screen. Water-soluble crayons, such as the Caran d'Ache brand, transfer to the screen very easily. You can use them directly on the screen either dry or dipped in water first. Not every mark will print, though; it will depend on how deeply the base penetrates the crayon. Try each material to see the result before making a print.

I add water to the transparent base before printing. You can experiment with different amounts. After the drawing is made, flood the screen (in the up position on the printing table) with base, moving back and forth over the screen. After you have let it sit for a minute or two, print it in register, but do not lift up the screen after printing. Instead, reflood it while it remains on the print and print it again. Sometimes I do this three or four times if the drawing is not printing to my satisfaction. After I remove the print, I flood the screen again and print on another piece of paper. As you might expect, each monoprint is weaker than the one before. The two or three prints you obtain can be used as a ground for another image. It is rare to be totally satisfied with the monoprint per se. Most artists add other printings on top of the first image.

During the printing process, the base will become tinted by the colors from the screen. It is necessary to change it frequently, otherwise the areas on the print that should remain clear will pick up this diluted color mixture.

Many of the results of this method are unpredictable. If the crayon line is too dense, it will act as a resist to the transparent base, and only the edges will print. This gives the line a unique and beautiful quality. Several printings on different pieces of paper will eventually remove the line from the screen. This makes the prints uniquely different from each other.

I find that the color of the crayons is limited; when they are used exclusively, the color is too "sweet." The combination of watercolor and gouache with the crayons changes that and allows the artist to create more complex and exciting colors with a complete palette.

Moreover, watercolor and gouache alone, without the crayon, create interesting images.

Experimentation pays off in monoprinting. For example, watercolor can be painted in a thick and dry consistency, or in a thin and wet consistency. The base can be left on the screen for a few minutes or a few seconds. The crayon can be painted on a dry screen or one that is already flooded with base. There is no correct way, and familiarizing yourself with different results gives you greater flexibility in creating desired effects, particularly in representational works.

There are limitations, however, on how long the base can sit on the screen before printing. The watercolor or gouache can dry on the screen, but once you flood it with base, it must be printed after a minute or two. I have also sprayed the underside of a screen to wet the image and loosen up the paint. This is tricky, for the water must be contained within the borders of the image.

A series of monoprints was made by the artist Darra Keeton. She spent two weeks at the Screenprint Workshop and created a series of thirteen final prints. Each one was developed with more than one printing. The very light printings—almost ghost images—of previous prints formed the basis for half of the prints. Ms. Keeton would work on the screen with crayon and paint and print it onto three or four pieces of paper. Sometimes she liked it and sometimes she did not. The ones she liked she set aside to continue in the direction she started. The others she printed over with entirely different designs.

The results were always exciting and surprising. She shared her feelings about the process with me: "Every medium has its particular restrictions as well as its freedoms, and I like shifting from one to another as I develop my images. For me, the beauty of screened water-based monoprints is the possibility of having fluid and mannered marks, as in watercolor, in which you can work either quickly and spontaneously, or carefully and slowly. The most fun comes in working directly on the screen, making rapid decisions

MONOPRINTING:

With the screen set up on blocks, a rectangular shape of open mesh has been made with photo emulsion. The mesh that the artist is working on has been printed several times, and the stain of the previous drawings is visible. The mixture that is painted on here is white and yellow gouache mixed with transparent base.

The artist Darra Keeton is drawing on the screen while it is still wet and in register.

The print is studied by the artist after the color has been printed.

Keeton confers with the printer on the next possibility for this print. It was printed twice more and became the third monoprint in the series.

These are five monoprints that Dara Keeton made over a two-week period at the Screenprint Workshop. Each of them has had several printings.

Print #1 was made with one drawn layer of Caran d'Ache water-soluble crayon, one middle layer of painted gouache, and a last layer of orange, drawn on with crayon again.

Print #2 was made over a weaker, ghost-image version of Print #1. Two layers of gouache and watercolor were printed on top.

Print #3 is the final result of the print that the artist and printer conferred about. It had three ghost images of other printings (not of #1 and #2). Dark Caran d'Ache crayons were used to form the organic shape, and the last layer was gouache.

Print #4 had the most printings and was almost abandoned by the artist. Two ghost images and three layers of gouache were finished off with a last printing of orange crayon.

Print #8 was based on ghost images of #1 and #6 with an overall printing of ultramarine blue watercolor. The last color was a white gouache that the artist allowed to dry into the screen, causing it to resist the printing and produce a beautiful white pattern on the top of the shape.

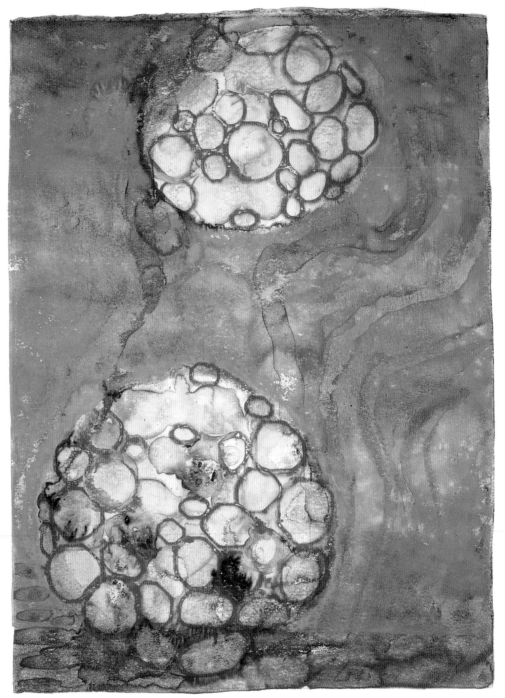

PRINT #1

before the transparent base dries. I love the fact that I can work directly without the image being reversed, as it would be on an etching press."

Cleaning Up
After a drawing is printed a few times, the screen should be cleaned. Using a spatula or scoop card, remove the base and keep it in a container with a secure top. This base can be used to mix colors. Wash out the screen with the spray water bottle and paper towels. The ghost image or stain of the drawing will remain in the screen. This is very helpful in the beginning if you want to continue adding color to the same image. After many different images have been drawn, a given image will be confusing and difficult to see. Remove the screen and scrub it with cleanser to get some of the stain out. It will not get perfectly clear, but will be fine for drawing on again.

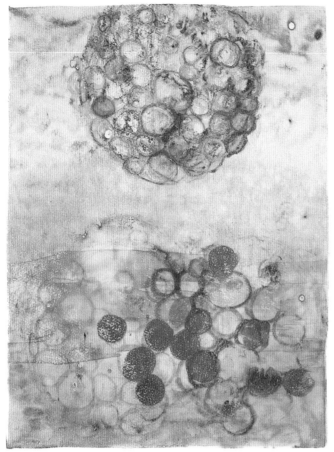

PRINT #2

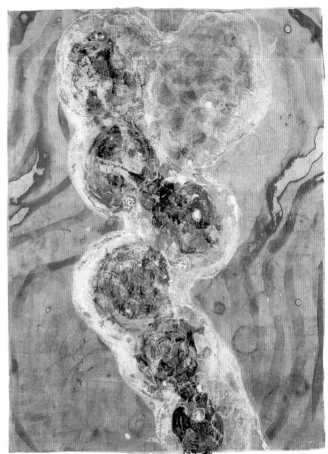

PRINT #3

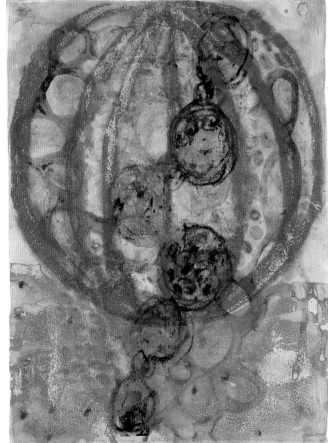

PRINT #4

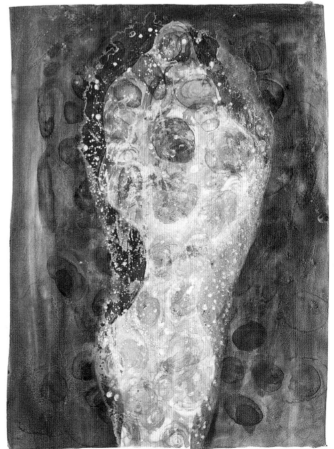

PRINT #8

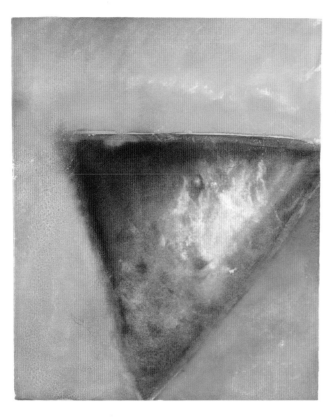
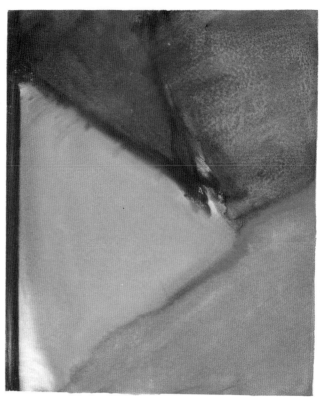
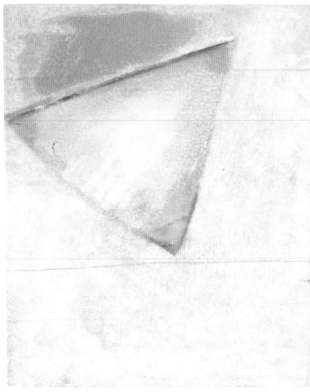
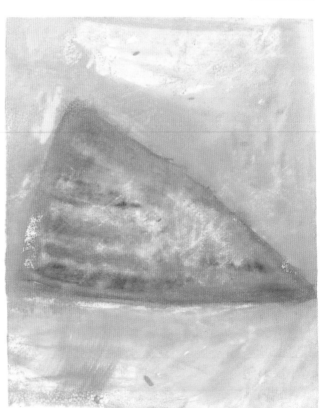

This set of four monoprints
was printed by Dawn Henning-
Santiago with watercolor and
transparent base.

 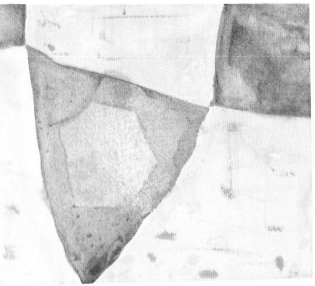

Two different states: One shows the first printing, and the other shows the second printing, the "ghost." Both versions were made by Dawn Henning-Santiago.

Roni Henning, *Daisy*, 14 x 25" (35.5 x 63.5 cm). This realistic rabbit monoprint was made by the author with watercolor and water-soluble crayons.

Chapter 8

Cleanup of Inks and Stencils

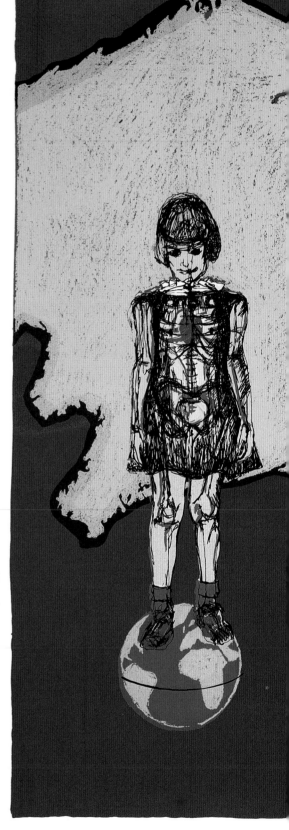

For years, when I printed with oil-based inks, I always dreaded the cleanup phase of the job. It involved noisy exhaust fans, heavy gloves, and sometimes respirators. I hated the prospect of leaning over the screen and breathing the fumes from the solvents. Even when cleanup was no longer anything that I did personally, the shop would always smell of solvents and ink. On the following pages, the water-based system is shown to liberate the screenprinter from these headaches. Removal of inks from screens and reclaiming screens—an essential moneysaver—become fuss-free.

Susan Spencer Crowe, *American Girl*, 30 x 22" (76.2 x 56 cm).
The print, published by Avocet in 1991, was printed by Andrea
Collard and Susan Spencer Crowe in seven colors using Createx
water-based inks. All the screens were reclaimed with Holden's
emulsion remover and a pressure hose.

INK REMOVAL

Cleaning up water-based inks is almost a pleasure, especially when reclaiming screens for reuse in dozens of printings.

WASHOUT STAND
HOSE WITH SPRAY-NOZZLE ATTACHMENT
FLOOR FAN
PLASTIC WATER BOTTLE WITH A SPRAY TOP
PAPER TOWELS
INK SPATULA OR CARDBOARD SCOOP CARDS
THIN PLASTIC GLOVES (SURGICAL)

As soon as your last sheet of paper is printed and racked, place a piece of newspaper under the screen. Do not flood the screen, but immediately spray it with water, making sure to wet the open mesh of the stencil area first. This will keep the mesh open and prevent the ink from drying during cleaning. Some ink companies recommend a chemical that they supply to be sprayed into the screen to prevent the ink from bonding to the mesh. I have never found this necessary, but if you do, International Chemical Company's 884 is a relatively nontoxic one.

Using a spatula or scoop card, remove all the excess ink from the screen and return it to the container. If it is too hard or lumpy and cannot be used to make other colors, discard it. I usually try to keep a tiny amount of each color, in case some touch-up is necessary during the inspection of the finished edition. Also, scrape all the ink from each side of the squeegee. All the while, continue spraying the screen with water.

There are two methods of washing the ink from the screen.

Using a Washout Stand

If you have a print shop or studio with a waste-water drain that connects to a sewer system, the screen can be cleaned in a washout stand. This washout stand is similar or identical to the one described in Chapter 4, on screen preparation. It is usually made of metal with a high back and sides. The front looks like a trough. Alongside the stand, have a hose with a spray nozzle connected to the water supply. Place the screen in the washout stand and wash the ink thoroughly away on both sides with the hose. Stubborn areas can be scrubbed with a stiff nylon brush and some form of household cleanser such as Ajax. When all the ink is removed, dry the screen in front of a floor fan.

Washing to Conserve Water

When the need to conserve water is very important—as it is in my shop, the Screenprint Workshop—a screen may be cleaned on the printing table. The Screenprint Workshop does not connect to a sewer system, so our waste water must be kept from contaminating the ground water.

I follow the same procedure already outlined, up to and including scraping the ink from the screen. Then, using paper towels and the spray water bottle, I wash the screen on the table, making sure to put a newspaper under the open stencil. I always wear gloves; though the ink is water-based, it is advisable to keep it from getting into your nails and pores. No ink or paint is totally nontoxic, otherwise we would be able to eat it.

Work in a precise and orderly way. I always fold a number of paper towels before I start. This makes the job faster and easier. After all the excess ink has been removed from the screen, spray it thoroughly using the water bottle. With the towels, wipe up the ink on the sides of the screen around the open mesh of the stencil. This will get the bulk of the ink up so you won't be pulling it into the open mesh. Repeat this until most of the ink is gone.

Change the paper towels as soon as they are full of ink; don't keep rubbing them back and forth across the screen. Now clean the open mesh area. Constantly spray with water. Change the newspaper under the screen once it becomes saturated and replace it with a clean one.

Once the inside of the screen is fairly clean, lift it up and spray and clean the underside of the screen. Wash it until the paper towels don't pick up any more ink. There may be a stain of the color ink that was printed. This is only a stain; the screen will still be clean and reusable. Remove the screen from the table and dry it with the fan.

Make sure to wash the spatula and squeegee when you are finished. This can be done in the washout stand or with water and paper towels.

1

1. Once your printing is done, newspaper is placed under the screen.

2. The screen is sprayed with water to prevent ink from drying in the mesh.

3. The excess ink is scraped from the screen with a metal spatula.

4. After spraying the screen thoroughly with water, wipe the ink out of the screen with paper towels.

5. When the inside of the screen is clean, the underside is sprayed and wiped with paper towels.

6. The screen is placed in a washout stand, and the ink is washed off with water. This method can be used if the waste water washes into a sewer system.

2

3

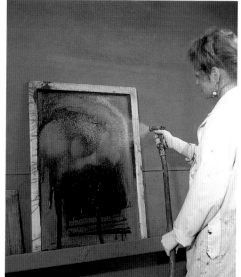

4

5

6

RECLAIMING SCREENS:

1. Bleach is applied to a screen on both sides with a sponge. Gloves should be worn when using bleach.

2. The screen is covered with newspaper and sprayed with more bleach to keep it wet. It is left on the screen for fifteen to twenty minutes.

3. The emulsion is washed out of the screen with a garden hose and hot water after the newspaper is removed.

1

2

3

RECLAIMING SCREENS

The sooner the photo emulsion is removed after printing, the better, for it will continue to harden. The screens at the Screenprint Workshop are all kept in racks under a yellow safelight. This ensures that the hardening process is slowed down until they are cleaned.

MATERIALS

WASHOUT STAND
WATER HOSE OR HIGH-PRESSURE WASHER
BLEACH OR EMULSION REMOVER
VINEGAR

My print workshop uses a washout stand to reclaim screens, but all the waste water is collected in a container that is attached to the washout stand. I use several different methods in reclaiming screens, depending upon the needs of the print shop. I use either a high-pressure washer or a garden hose.

High-Pressure Washer

Place the screen in the washout stand. Wearing gloves and using a sponge, apply a coat of bleach to both sides. Allow the bleach to remain on the screen for two to three minutes. It will start to break down the emulsion. A high-pressure washer is a separate unit that is connected to the water system. A pump forces the water out of the hose with heavy pressure that strips the emulsion from the screen very quickly.

Garden Hose

Most emulsion manufacturers also sell emulsion removers. These products usually have some toxic materials that it is better to avoid. However, there are chemical companies that have been making emulsion removers that have a nontoxic rating. One of them, a product called 833, is manufactured by the International Chemical Corporation. This remover is citrus-based. It is applied to the screen on both sides with a sponge or spray bottle. When the emulsion starts to dissolve, wash it using hot water and a hose in a washout stand. This can be repeated for stubborn spots.

If the emulsion remover is unavailable, use bleach. It may be necessary to soak the screen with bleach covered with paper towels or newspaper and allow it to sit for about twenty minutes.

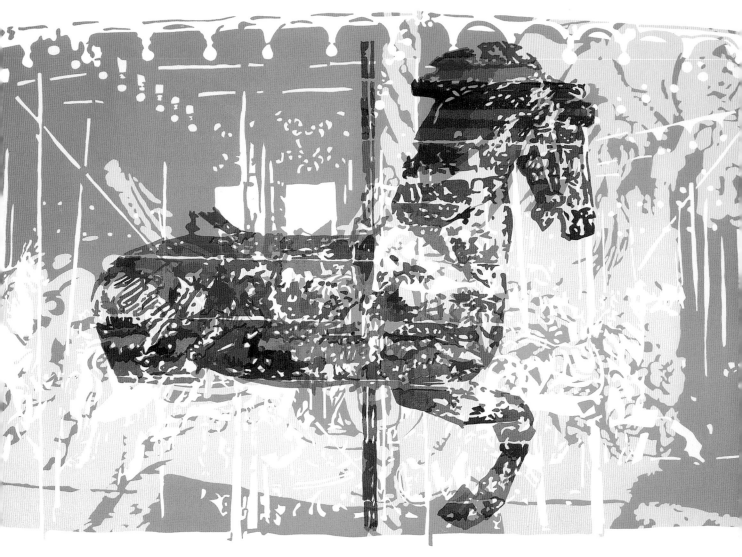

Make sure the bleach does not dry on the screen. Every time a chemical dries on a screen, it combines with what is already left on the screen; emulsion and ink residues will bond with other materials and make them even more difficult to remove. If needed, you can sandwich the screen between rags or paper towels soaked with bleach in order to keep the screen wet. Interestingly enough, if the emulsion was not sufficiently hardened on the screen during exposure, it will be more difficult to reclaim.

In the washout stand, using a garden hose with a spray nozzle and hot water, wash the emulsion out of the screen. Wash it on both sides until it is clean. Again, what will remain on the screen is a ghost image of the color that was just printed. This is merely a stain that will not interfere with the application of another stencil.

Once it appears that nothing more will come out of the screen, remove it from the stand and dry it in front of a floor fan. If the screen has some remaining stubborn spots, these can be scrubbed out with an abrasive cleanser and a stiff nylon brush. Work both sides of the screen at the same time. If it is a large screen, you need two people. Most professional print shops rely on acetone as a final cleaner to remove hard spots. I try to limit the use of acetone; it is a toxic chemical with harmful fumes.

The last step is to neutralize the screen with acetic acid, which is found in vinegar. Apply this to both sides of the screen with a sponge and then wash it with water one last time. The screen is now ready for a new stencil. The stencils for Joe Testa-Secca's *Relic* were shot on screens that had been reclaimed at least fifty times.

Joe Testa-Secca, *Relic*, 22 x 30" (56 x 76.2 cm). Printed at the Screenprint Workshop by the author, this work was done with T.W. Graphics inks mixed with transparent base. The screens were reclaimed with International Chemical Corporation's 833 emulsion remover.

Chapter 9

Creating a Safer Print Shop

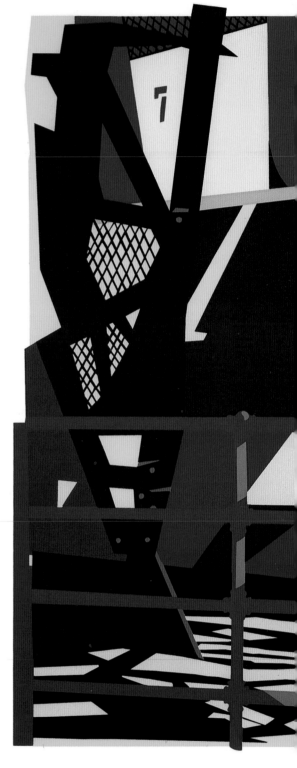

I realize that recycling, water conservation, and garbage disposal must be cost-effective for large commercial print shops to be interested. The amount of time that it takes employees to peel paint from ink containers and rewash acetate will be weighed against what the employer considers a productive use of a worker's time. But, having worked in large oil-based print shops, I've seen the amount of unnecessary waste. The time taken to recycle and reuse many supplies will be made up by the savings from not continually replenishing these items.

Philomena Marano,
This Way Out,
29 1/2 x 41" (75 x 104 cm).
This work had been printed with
oil-based inks in 1988 before
I switched to water. Later, the
Rubylith stencils were stripped of
the red film and the clear acetates
were used to make overlays for
other separations.

RECYCLING

Obviously, when a print shop is very busy, that is not the time to be cleaning off acetates. But all shops have slow periods, and it is at this time when the recycling can be done. As the list below shows, there are by-products of printing that ought to be considered.

Acetate

When acetate sheets are used to make stencils for color separations, they serve a purpose. At the end of an edition these stencils are usually tossed in the garbage. Collect the used acetates and keep them on a specific shelf or box for future use. Most of the material used to paint on the stencils, such as lithographer's opaque, is water-soluble. Wash the sheets with soap and water. Household cleansers like Ajax and steel wool will remove the litho crayon and stubborn marks.

Rubylith or Amberlith Film

These films are a little harder to recycle. It all depends on how much cutting has been done to each piece. An overall cut square can easily be recut for another job, but pieces that have a lot of detail, like the stencils for Philomena Morano's print *This Way Out*, are not easy to reuse. In those cases, I peel the remaining red film off and use the clear plastic for overlay sheets when I figure out the separations for a new print. I also use them to connect pieces of acetate or Rubylith, in order to extend them into a bigger sheet.

Products Used	Waste Generated
Acetate and Rubylith film	Acetate sheets and scrap
Inks	Excess ink
Ink containers	Used ink containers
Emulsion	Empty emulsion cans
Paper, newsprint	Leftover prints, proofed paper
Paper, sold by the box	Empty corrugated boxes
Developers and fixative	Used developer and fixative
Tape (masking and cellophane)	Scrap tape

Ink

Often when mixing a color to match the original art, I overmix. This gives me an excess amount of ink. I find that these mixtures can be used for other print jobs. I keep them in tightly closed containers and label them or tape a color swatch to the outside of the containers to identify the ink.

When a color is printed, there is usually some ink left over, and that combined with the residue scraped from the screen in cleaning can also be used to combine with other inks to make new colors. This is only possible if the ink is still soluble and has not gotten dried out or lumpy in the printing process.

During the color-mixing process, many ink containers are emptied of their color. These dirty containers are usually plastic. Reusing these saves buying new empty ones for mixing ink. Because the water-based ink is some form of plastic-derivative, it can be easily cleaned out. Of course, rinsing the containers with water is one possibility, but if water conservation is an issue, just let the residue of ink dry and it will peel out of the container. I also reuse the plastic buckets that the photo emulsion comes in.

Of course, empty cans and jars can be collected and returned to a local recycling center.

Paper

One of the largest supplies in the print shop is paper—paper to print on and cleanup paper, like newsprint. When making an edition of prints, there is always an extra number of sheets of paper beyond the exact number in the edition. For example, to get an edition of fifty prints, sixty-five are printed. That gives you fifteen extra prints to allow for errors. For an edition of 100, you print 125, and so on. These extra misprints become just so much garbage after the edition is made. Collect all this extra printed material and, instead of using new newsprint, use it on future jobs to test the way the screen prints: it always takes a few pieces of paper to get the screen printing smoothly each time a new color is printed.

There becomes a point when reused paper is saturated, and I then use it one more time when I clean the ink out of the screen. Then, finally, I'm ready to discard it as garbage.

Of course, I also collect old newspapers to be used in cleaning ink out of the screen.

When I order paper for an edition, I have it precut to the size that the artist wants the print to be. When the paper is delivered to the shop, it is carefully packaged in cartons of corrugated cardboard. These cartons are unpacked and stored. I repack the boxes with the printed edition, thus eliminating the need for purchasing extra cardboard.

Used Developer and Fixative

All the developer and fixative that is left over in the darkroom is collected in a tank. This tank has an evaporation system that removes the liquid. The silver that is left in the bottom of the tank is then retrieved. There are many environmental companies that will set up a system that will fit the needs of most shops. Shop around for the best available price.

Scrap Tape

Unfortunately, I can find no use for tape once it has been used. I just try to be as frugal as possible.

WATER CONSERVATION

Although water is a replenishable resource, it is still necessary to conserve it. Conservation reduces the amount of waste water that is generated in a water-based print shop. Even following the steps outlined in Chapter 8, on reclaiming screens, there is still a substantial amount of waste water left over from making and cleaning screens. If your shop or studio is hooked up to a city sewer system, then the waste water is automatically treated at a sewerage disposal plant. However, if it is not, as at the Screenprint Workshop, there are limited choices:

1. Collect the waste water in 50-gallon drums and have it collected periodically by an environmental company that treats it ($500 for each drum).

2. Install a water treatment system that allows the water to be run through carbon filters to remove the impurities.

3. The Screenprint Workshop works with an environmental consultant to

Mixed colors from previous prints are put in recycled containers and color-swatched for easy identification.

Below: When the residue of ink that is left in the container dries, it is easily removed by peeling it away.

This is an array of empty containers that have been cleaned to use for mixing new colors.

develop a system of recycling the waste water to use in reclaiming the screens. This system will use a pressure hose to strip the emulsion more efficiently. The water will drain from the washup stand into a large container to be used again. While the water is not being used, the emulsion sediment will settle to the bottom and be pumped out into another container for disposal. This will cut down on the amount of waste to be generated. Only at the end of the cleaning will a final rinse of fresh water be needed.

All these choices involve commercial companies that either set up a system or cart away the waste water. This is again an incentive to conserve.

GARBAGE DISPOSAL

Even with recycling there is still a good amount of garbage in a print shop. Paper towels are one of the biggest items. Since they are used to clean the ink from the screen, they are very hard to reuse. I only use paper towels that are made from recycled paper.

Sponges can be used instead of paper towels to wash the ink out of the screen. For me, the conflict is always whether to fill up the garbage dump or add more waste water. The sponges must be washed and waste water is one of my biggest concerns. Clean cotton rags can also be used for washing, and they can be cleaned. I try to keep my garbage confined to paper products; fortunately, all containers are plastic or glass and can be recycled.

Commercial print shops have their garbage collected by commercial garbage companies. This garbage is then removed to the local dump for disposal. Each town has its own ordinance as to the disposal of toxic material. Printed paper and water-based inks can be considered hazardous waste, if they contain heavy metals, and must be treated accordingly.

SAFETY

Working with water-based inks has eliminated most of the fumes from the shop. This makes it unnecessary to install exhaust systems. However, you are still using ink that is basically pigment suspended in some form of polymer base. Some brands still contain metals, and all the manufacturers' warnings and instructions should be followed.

I always use gloves when mixing ink or cleaning ink out of the screen. The gloves that I use are very thin surgical gloves that do not interfere with the printing procedures. The gloves that I formerly used with oil-based inks and solvents were of thick plastic and were very unwieldy. They would last less than a week and eventually deteriorate. That proves how caustic the chemicals were; they could be absorbed into a heavy plastic glove in five or six days. I never allow food around the ink and, of course, there's no smoking.

As an artist and printmaker, my only concern with supplies is in relation to the result I wanted to achieve in my art. Could I make a print brighter, more opaque, or glossier? I would experiment with almost anything to get a different technique. Today, because I'm older and wiser, I rarely use anything with such total abandon. The world, it seems, has also become older and wiser and more aware of its diminishing resources.

One of the advertisements that I received from Tower Chemical Company began: "Join the many passengers on board the Noncarcinogenic Safety Train." It went on to state: "Today's printer wants maximum productivity and product value, but is concerned about chemical safety and compliance with OSHA's hazard communication laws." This company, observing the guidelines of the federal Occupational Safety and Health Agency (OSHA), was specializing in replacing more hazardous chemicals in pressrooms with safer, efficient alternatives. Although this company's chemistry was not applicable for my purposes, it proved that the industry was at last seeking comparable alternatives to their more toxic products. This new focus by manufacturers has made it possible to create prints that satisfy the creative needs of artists without diminished quality or enormous health risks to the printers.

I recommend that you always examine each item in the print shop individually. Since solvents are eliminated, the two major areas of concern are inks and emulsions.

Opposite page: Gladys Burrows, *Studio Window*, 22½ x 17⅝" (57.2 x 44.7 cm). The colors were derived from mixtures that were saved from other printings. This was an edition of 300, printed by the author at the Screenprint Workshop.

Inks

Each brand of ink comes with its own materials safety data sheet. This information can help you make a safer choice. Some ink retarders are more toxic than others for different brands. In Chapter 5, I have listed a sampling of water-based inks, and suppliers are listed in the Appendix.

Some companies are more helpful than others in answering questions. For instance, Mr. Dick Kelsey of T.W. Graphics, in California, has been very forthcoming with information about the ingredients and safety of that company's products. It is also possible to speak to the chemists of the ink manufacturers. I was able, for instance, to speak directly with Mr. Al Spizzo of Hunt Manufacturing Company, the makers of Hunt's Speedball ink.

The Boston-based Art and Craft Materials Institute, which tests different products to see the levels of toxicity, will also send information on any of the products tested. Their address is 715 Boylston Street, Boston, MA 02116.

Emulsion

Emulsions still remain one of the more toxic items in the shop, because they contain diazo, a harmful chemical. Always wear gloves when using emulsions, and never wash them away so that they will end up in the ground water. Check the materials safety data sheet of the emulsion remover, obtainable from the manufacturer (see the sample safety data sheet, pp. 138-139), and a reference guide that explains the symbols on the data sheet is available from The Department of Environmental Health and Safety, State University of New York at Stony Brook, Long Island, New York.

Of course, you can use removers that are listed as nontoxic, such as International Chemical Company's 833 emulsion remover. Bleach works well, but be careful—it can burn your skin.

Opposite page:
The next wave: The color separations for this image were created with a computer. Printed at Noblet Serigraphic, Inc., New York.

Below:
Karen Gray, *Three Ladies*, 22 x 30" (56 x 76.2 cm). Printed by the author and Greg Radich at the Screenprint Workshop.

INTERCONTINENTAL CHEMICAL CORPORATION

4660 Spring Grove Ave., Cincinnati, Ohio 45232 513-541-7100

MATERIAL SAFETY DATA SHEET

PRODUCT IDENTIFICATION.   ICC 833   (07/13/90)

HAZARDOUS INGREDIENTS.
   ICC 833 is not a hazardous product.

03: PHYSICAL DATA.
   Initial Boiling Point: ~7E216° F.   Vapor Pressure: ~7EWater.
   Water Soluble: Complete.   Percent Volatile: >55.
   Vapor Density: >1 (Air = 1)   Specific Gravity: >1.
   Odor: Sight.   Appearance: Clear liquid.
   SCAQMD Rule 1130: 0.0#/gallon; Og/l   Initial Evaporation Rate: ~7EWater.

04: FIRE AND EXPLOSION HAZARD DATA.
   Non-Flammable (Title 29 CFR 1910.106).
   Flammable Limits: Not applicable.   Flash Point: None.
   Extinguishing Media: Not applicable   Fire Hazards: None.
   No Special Fire Fighting Procedures
   NFPA 704 Code System Rating: **Health 0;   Flammability 0;   Reactivity 0.**

05: HEALTH HAZARD DATA.
   Non-Toxic (when used according to directions).
   No Carcinogenic Compounds (IARC; NTP; OSHA).

   Overexposure may cause irritation to eyes; skin; nose; and mouth.

   First Aid Procedure:
      Eyes: Flush with water.
      Skin: Rinse with water.
      Inhalation: Remove to fresh air.
      Ingestion: Rinse mouth. Drink water or milk.

06: REACTIVITY DATA.
   No Photochemically Reactive Solvents.
   Stability: Stable
   Incompatibility: Not observed.
   Conditions to Avoid: Welding arcs.
   Hazardous Polymerization: Cannot occur.
   Hazardous Decomposition: Burning may produce CO and CO_2.

07: SPILL OR LEAK PROCEDURES.
   Drain-Safe (when used in accordance with directions).
   No Petroleum Solvents or Derivatives.
   Spilled material may be wiped with rags or mop. Larger quantities may
      be flushed with water, and if available, squeegeed to drain.

08: CONTROL MEASURES.
   No special equipment requirement. Adequate ventilation, splash-proof
      goggles and chemical-resistant gloves are recommended for use when han-
      dling any chemical.

09: PRECAUTIONS FOR SAFE HANDLING AND STORAGE
   Containers should be kept closed when not in use. Product should not be
      contaminated with other material. Containers stored outdoors should have
      bungs closed and protective covering; avoid storing in standing water. Do
      not reuse container.

10: REGULATORY INFORMATION
   ICC 833 contains no chemicals that are subject to the reporting
      requirements of SARA Title III, Section 313 and 40 CFR 372.

INTERCONTINENTAL CHEMICAL CORPORATION believes that the data
contained herein are factual and the opinions expressed are those of qualified
experts. The data are not to be taken as a representation for which Intercontinental
Chemical Corporation assumes legal responsibility. They are offered for your
consideration and verification.

ICC 833   07/13/90

Suppliers

CREATEX
14 Airport Park Road
East Granby, CT 06026

Pure pigments and Lyntex screenprinting base.

DIRECT REPRODUCTIONS
Box 150585
Brooklyn, NY 11215-0006

Textured acetate.

E & A SCREEN GRAPHICS
48-85 Maspeth Avenue
Maspeth, NY 11378

Total photo-positive services and manufacturing of screenprinting screens.

HUNT MANUFACTURING COMPANY
Speedball Road
Statesville, NC 28677

Hunt's Speedball water-soluble screenprinting ink.

INTERCONTINENTAL CHEMICAL CORPORATION
4660 Spring Grove Avenue
Cincinnati, OH 45232

Emulsion removers and retarders.

LEXAN (DIVISION OF GE PLASTICS)
One Plastics Avenue
Pittsville, MA 01201

A variety of textured Lexan films.

NEW YORK CENTRAL
62 Third Avenue
New York, NY

Screenprinting supplies and paper. A licensed dealer of T.W. Graphics water-based inks.

PEARL PAINT
308 Canal Street
New York, NY 10013

Screenprinting supplies and paper.

SAVOIR-FAIRE
Box 2021
Sausalito, CA 94966

Lascaux paints, water-based screenprinting paste, and fine-art paper.

T.W. GRAPHICS
7220 East Slauson Avenue
City of Commerce, CA 90040

A complete water-based ink selection, plus all screenprint materials and equipment.

ULANO CORPORATION
255 Butler Street
Brooklyn, NY 11217

Photo emulsions and masking film (Rubylith and Amberlith).

UNION INK COMPANY, INC.
463 Broad Avenue
Ridgefield, NJ 07657

Water-soluble Echo print ink.

Bibliography

Biegeleisen, J.I.: *Silk Screen Printing Production*, Dover Publications, N.Y., 1963.

Carr, Francis: *Screen Printing*, Vista Books, London, 1961.

Faine, Brad: *The Complete Guide to Screenprinting*, Quarto Publishing, London, 1989.

Lassiter, Frances and Norman: *Screen Printing: Contemporary Methods and Materials*, Hunt Manufacturing Co., Philadelphia, 1978.

Saff, Donald, and Deli Sacilotto, *Screenprinting: History and Process*, Holt, Rinehart and Winston, New York, 1979.

Glossary

Acetate: a plastic material, a sheet of which is drawn or painted upon to make color separations.

Amberlith: an orange-colored transparent film attached to a plastic backing and used to make knife-cut stencils.

C print: a color photo made from an original.

Chop mark: the individual logo of the printer that is embossed into an edition.

Color separation: a means of putting the various colors of an image onto plates or positives that are then made into stencils on a screen.

Continuous tone: the effect gained from the blending of one color into another, or of black into white.

Copy board: the place on the process camera where the original picture or art is placed.

Deckle: the ragged edge on handmade paper.

Degrease: to remove the oily film on fabrics and acetates.

Developer: the photo chemical in which film is placed after it has been exposed; consequently, the image that was copied appears on the film.

Direct stencil: a screen created by means of blocking areas of the fabric to allow the ink to print through the nonblocked, open areas.

Dot screen: a uniform dot pattern on a plastic sheet that is used in making halftone positives.

Drying rack: an apparatus consisting of shelves where wet prints are placed to dry.

Durometer: the hardness or softness of the squeegee.

Edition: a specific number of identical prints made of one image and signed and numbered by the artist.

Fixative: the photo chemical that makes the picture on the film permanent.

Flood: to push ink into the mesh of a screen before printing it on the paper.

Foamcore: a lightweight board.

Gloss: the shiny surface of a printed ink.

Gouache: opaque watercolor.

Halftone: a printed image made by breaking a continuous-tone image, usually a photograph, into opaque dots.

Halide light: an ultraviolet light used to expose screens coated with photo emulsion.

Illustration board: a stiff white cardboard used to paint or draw on.

Indirect stencil: a stencil made of a material that is applied to the screen with a photo emulsion.

Lithographic wash: the simulation of a painted wash in a printed image, created by the lithographic method.

Lithography: a printing method in which an image is drawn on flat stones or metal plates and transferred by pressure onto paper.

Maquette: a small original used as a model for the final print.

Mat knife: a sharp knife with a razor-like blade in a handle, commonly used to cut mats for picture frames.

Matte: a flat (as opposed to glossy) surface of printed ink.

Mesh: a fine network of woven fibers with small holes between the threads.

Mezzotint: an image made with a random dot pattern; also, the plastic sheet that contains the random dot pattern used to make photo-positive stencils.

Monofilament: a single thread; a fabric woven from single threads, used for screens in screenprinting.

Monoprint: an image made in a one-time printing process.

Multifilament: a thread of many strands twisted together; a fabric woven from such threads, used for screens in screenprinting.

Negative: an image showing the dark areas on a photographic film as light and the light areas as dark; the reverse of positive.

Off-contact: the release of the screen from the paper during printing, because the screen is not resting flat on the table.

One-arm squeegee: a bar and handle to which the squeegee is attached that runs perpendicular to the back of the printing table.

Orthochromatic film: a high-contrast film that is used to copy a picture.

Painted wash: a term for paint applied in a thin, translucent layer with modulations like those of a watercolor.

Photo emulsion: a light-sensitive material that is coated onto a screen to make a stencil.

Photoflood bulb: a source of intense light used by photographers to illuminate their subject.

Photosensitive: a term applied to any photographic material that reacts to light.

Pochoir: the French word for stencil.

Pointillism: a system of painting developed primarily by the artist Georges Seurat, in which dots of different colors are placed next to each other to make an image.

Positive: the correct—as opposed to the reversed, or negative—appearance of the darks and lights in an image; also, a color separation for screenprinting.

Posterization: a stencil-making process that employs different time exposures of one image to make several photo-positive stencils; the step-progression printing of an image from such stencils.

Printing table: a table to which a screen is attached for printing.

Process copy camera: a camera used to copy pictures onto photo-positive film for printing.

Proofing: the practice of testing the stencils and colors of a print before making an edition.

Reclaim: to clean a screen by removing all the inks and stencils so that it can be used again.

Reduction printing: a system of printing whereby the open area of the screen is blocked or reduced every time a color is printed.

Registration: a method of ensuring that separations line up with each other and that colors print in exactly the same place on each sheet of paper.

Retarder: an additive that slows the drying of ink.

Rubylith: a red-colored transparent film attached to a plastic backing and used to make knife-cut stencils.

Safelight: a reddish light under which light-sensitive photographic paper can be processed in a darkroom.

Screen: a wooden or metal frame that is covered with a fabric mesh, used to make screenprints.

Screen filler: a liquid substance used to paint out an area on a screen so that ink cannot pass through it.

Screenprinting: a printing method that produces prints by pushing ink through a screen with a squeegee.

Scoop cards: pieces of cardboard or illustration board that are used to remove ink or excess emulsion from a screen.

Scoop coater: a tool used to apply photo emulsion to a screen.

Solvent: a toxic chemical used to thin oil-based inks and to reclaim screens.

Squeegee: the tool used to push ink through the mesh of a screen to print an image.

Stop bath: the chemical in which photographic film is placed in order to stop the development process.

Trapping: the slight overlapping of printed colors so that unprinted paper does not show between color areas.

Vacuum frame exposure unit: the equipment that holds a coated screen in tight contact with a positive for exposure.

Viscosity: the thickness or thinness of the ink; also, the ink's sticky quality.

Index